Terrence,

   May you be blessed in your marriage. Honor this in all that you do and your life will be richly blessed.

   K. B.

Living In Autumn While Preparing for *Spring*

The Journey Towards Marriage

WRITTEN BY

Karen C. Bowlding

Living In Autumn While Preparing for *Spring*

The Journey Towards Marriage

PUBLISHED BY

The Vineyard, LLC

Published by:
The Vineyard, LLC
P.O. Box 478
Upper Marlboro, Maryland 20773
www.thevineyard-books.com

Unless otherwise noted, all Scripture quotations are from The NIV Study Bible, 10th Anniversary Edition New International Version Zondervan Publishing House Grand Rapids, Michigan 49530 USA copyright ©1985, 1995, 2002

Book Layout & Design and editing by:
VBP OutSourcing, Inc
www.vbpoutsourcing.com

Cover Models: Darryl & Lisa Richards

Library of Congress control number: 2005932788
ISBN 0-9773805-0-5

Printed in the United States of America October 2005

To my husband Andre

Thank you for you enduring patience, insight, and help in putting this project together. You have encouraged, supported and given me the confidence to write this book. You are my friend, my lover, my pastor and my help. I love you with all my heart.

Acknowledgements

To my Heavenly Father

Father I thank you for the vision that you have given me. You have been with me the entire process, guiding, leading and instructing me. Your word and truth is the foundation of this book. You have shown your face throughout the project; helping me to push past fear and write what you would have me to write. I only hope that you are glorified.

To Bishop Deron and Pastor Jill Cloud

Deron and Jill your hard work was not in vain. I have learned a great deal from your experiences, the truths you have spoken and from your love. Your spiritual children are reproducing fruit after its own kind so be encouraged to continue the battle to make disciples of many. Thank you for answering the call on your lives. Countless lives are blessed because of you.

To my sister Kathy Anderson and dearest friend Tammy Richards

I appreciate your listening ear and words of encouragement.

Andre and I are grateful for the many couples and mentors that walked with us on our journey. Your wisdom, warnings and life stories provided us with a number of tools that kept us on track and helped us to remain centered in God. We would like to especially thank Rivion & Renee Johnson and Terrance & Dena Butler for continuing to be a blessing in our lives.

To all those that allowed me to tell their stories, I am thankful because I know others will be blessed because you freely shared your experiences.

A Personal Note from Andre

Life as a single Christian male was an excellent experience for me. I came and went as I pleased, my priorities were in order, there was no debt, and surprisingly enough no girlfriends, to overly concern myself with.

Arriving at this contentment in my life was not an easy process, nor did it take place overnight. It was a process that took sacrifice, trust, and faith.

Before I made the choice to serve God I was involved in a three year relationship that needed drastic change. We tried counseling but that didn't work too well. It eventually led us to try church. I can say we tried church and not God because that was all we knew. Our differences in desired teaching eventually lead us individually to different churches.

It was during this time that I really began to realize and notice my anger and insecurity problems. I knew that the relationship was about to end, which made my feelings of insecurity intensify. I detested that feeling like nothing I'd ever felt before in my life. I recall the evening distinctly after a special church service, feeling so jealous because of the attention from men that she received. I went home and cried furiously. I cried out to God, asking Him to take that feeling away from me. I needed Him like never before. Not only did He take that pain away that evening but He placed me in a church that helped me to acknowledge and get assistance with my insecurities and many other dysfunctional behaviors that stemmed from it. It is the acknowledgement of those problems that would allow me to be a more effective servant at my church and at work.

To care for others and to learn what love really was helped me to see women as people deserving admiration and honor as opposed to viewing them as sex objects. Additionally, I was able to submit to male authority without questioning their motives. Best of all I learned to be secure within myself which allowed me to be more nurturing and humorous with children, relating to them on their level, just having fun and being silly. I was no longer overly concerned about what people thought about me.

With that I became more focused on my job. I also enjoyed the nurturing relationships that came out of people wanting the same things I did, to grow, to change, and to enhance my spiritual life. I was able to separate myself from the people in my life who did not have my best interest in mind.

I truly believe that the one thing that sustained me through my single hood, my good and bad days, the successes and failures, was my core group of accountability partners. There were approximately ten of us men meeting bi-weekly to discuss any topic necessary, spiritual matters, marriage, children, and intimacy; no subject was off limits. The relationships that came out of this group remain and they're still useful and supportive.

I would say to every man that is in this type of gathering is essential. It doesn't matter what type of background you come from, everyone needs understanding and wisdom in some area in their lives that usually can be given by another. Far too often as men, pride doesn't allow us to come together in this fashion. So much of what we do and learn is tied to competition, to do and think better than the next. Of course competition has its' place but I believe too often we apply it improperly. Feelings of insecurity, inferiority, and envy oftentimes will not allow us as men to share information as well as ourselves. If you have the opportunity to be a part of such a group I hope that you take full advantage of it. I recommend that every man become involved in a small group that fosters such characteristics as compassion, kindness, accountability, patience and ultimately love.

A Personal Note from Karen

Since childhood, I had this fantasy of being married to my knight in shinning armor. I knew the type of person that I wanted and ideas of how the wedding ceremony would be. I thought that I would be so in love and that my husband would be nice to me, buy me things, and it would be a lot of fun. I saw marriage as dating that lasted forever, we would go out all the time and enjoy being with one another; I would never be alone. I didn't consider what a marriage relationship entailed. I thought that it would be easy because the man that I married would take care of me and give me what I wanted. I wished to be at home taking care of my husband and raising our children.

In my dating years I broke hearts and got my heart broken. I didn't realize it at the time, but it was all about me getting my desires met; my voids filled. I thought that sex meant that he liked me a whole lot, I wasn't even thinking about love. I dated many men; searching for something. If I only knew then what I know now, I could have saved myself a lot of trouble and heartache that came with my poor choices.

Because I lived carelessly in my 10 years of dating prior to accepting Christ, I did not expect to get married anytime soon, however, living single became a challenge for me the longer I was celibate, got older and watched several of my friends get married. Yes indeed, I struggled with lust. I hungered for physical touch and affection. I just wanted to be loved and have companionship. I wanted attention from a man; someone who cherished the ground that I walked on and treated me very well. I desired to be spoiled, told I was beautiful, sweet and smart. I became impatient with God. I wanted Him to move so that I would not be lonely. At that time I knew nothing about God's design for marriage.

I had my good days and bad ones. The better ones were when I enjoyed being single with no one to tell me what to do or having to answer to another. The unpleasant days came when someone became engaged or after I attended bridal showers and weddings ceremonies. At other times I had pity parties with my single girlfriends. I also checked out the guys at church to see who could be a potential mate; big mistake. At times, instead of being focused, my mind wandered and I daydreamed about men.

As the desire grew deep within me, I became sad, complaining and fussing with God. I was mad at Him for leaving me out. I became envious of others, especially worldly women because they could get any man they pleased while I had to be obedient. I often thought "why I couldn't have a man."

But, I didn't realize how unprepared I was for marriage. I still had many walls of protection around me. I wouldn't let anyone get that close to me yet. I was a runner – if a man got too close I rolled out of the relationship. Because I had not matured enough and known enough about me, no one else could know the real me either.

What helped me to make it through was a change of focus. I stopped being overly concerned about myself and began to focus more on God. My heart still desired marriage, but I had to keep living and not get consumed with the prospect. Because I worked in several ministries, I didn't have much time to dwell. I practically lived at church. My focused changed for a while, until someone told me they were engaged. I would then feel discontent for a few days and then get myself together.

Finally, I began to concentrate on dealing with my own issues. The more things I learned about myself, the more things I knew had to work on. I was so engrossed in becoming a person that God could be pleased with. I didn't conquer every area, but I worked hard on becoming a better person, one that was more compassionate, had a more grace with others and less critical and judgmental.

What I enjoyed about being single was the freedom of choice. I made decisions based upon what I needed at the time. I didn't have to weigh it against the desires of others. I liked going out and not answering to anyone. Sure I was accountable, but I lived for me. On the flip side, I didn't like having to do everything on my own either such as manage a home, pay bills, make critical decisions without a man's perspective, since they see things differently.

And just when I began to enjoy being single, Andre showed up.

Karen

Contents

The Current *Condition*

Many of us reading this book did not grow up a healthy home where both parents knew and loved the Lord wholeheartedly. We were not raised with Christian values, principles for living a righteous life, or have a true understanding of God's unfailing love and sacrifice of His son on our behalf. We were not guided or trained to live a life to honor the penalty that Christ paid for us. We grew up in dysfunctional families where a father may not have been present or did not operate in his God-given position as head of the household. Oftentimes, Momma ruled. Whatever she said went with no input from a male perspective. We were not taught to speak out against wrongdoing, confront bad behavior or offenses, forgive instead of holding grudges, go without justifying our point at the expense of another, or make the sacrifice for another. Never really understanding what was morally wrong or right in the first place, we followed the rules of the world. We learned that it was truly better to receive than to give. And then we met Jesus. Hallelujah!

The trend of today is to put off marriage as long as possible; to seek and conquer all who are willing first while sowing your wild oats until you have had your fill. A United States Census Bureau study (2000) revealed that the proportion of single men to women is 86 men for every 100 woman. Because there are many more women available for men, some carnal-minded men choose to date several women at a time or many women believing that with each subsequent partner they will eventually find perfection.

The problem with this is the longer you delay marriage, the more emotional baggage that develops. With each subsequent worldly relationship, the likelihood of chaos increase. When finally ready to marry, it will be harder to find one who is pure in heart, one who does not carry a host of emotional baggage, or one who does not come with tension from the other parent of their child or children. The longer one waits to marry, the harder it is to bring to an end the "I" focus and move into a "we" focused lifestyle.

Some men are not seeking a wife out of fear. They are waiting for a loud, booming voice from heaven telling them a certain woman is the exact one instead of walking in God's grace and free will that He has given them to find her. God will let you know if she is the "one" for you. Some men have become spiritually lazy, just not moving at all. They are waiting for a woman to approach them because they fear rejection. The excuses are plentiful for not finding a wife.

Marriage is not well-regarded in today's society. Television is now flooded with programs that completely devalue it. These programs make finding a wife a sport, a conquest of the flesh. The criteria are minimal and the relationships oftentimes do not make it to the altar. They are surface affairs created to bring in money. The couples on these television shows are not taking the time to get to know each other nor find out God's will. It is all about the illusion to fool viewers into believing that it is okay to play the field, date as many as possible until they think they have found the right one. The ratings for these programs are astronomical. We have lost the art of courting and romancing one person. Through these programs, young girls are now being taught that it is okay for a man to have many women at once, hoping that they will be the one that is chosen in the end. They are not taught to command respect from men. The men kiss every woman they encounter. These programs do not show after-taping antics. Who knows who is sleeping with the guy to put themselves in a better position to marry? Pun intended.

Dating is now described as someone with whom you are sleeping. No longer does the man seek God to find the mate destined for him. He only searches for what is visually pleasing. Women carelessly exchange their bodies for love, believing the lie that if they do not sleep with a man, they won't find true happiness and contentment. Because of the ratio of unmarried men to women, some women mistakenly believe that they should take what they can get because there are not enough available good men.

In dating, you don't know what you are getting into. You don't get to see the "real" person. Each partner is trying his best not to reveal his weaknesses or problems, while putting his best foot forward. Man's ways in this instance don't work. We should all know this from our own past experiences. As I look back on my ungodly life, no relationship worked. I ended up with sadness from a broken heart and other consequences from my actions. The difference now, walking in the light of Christ, is that I have freedom, peace of mind, and a healthy God-centered relationship with my husband.

Being single is not a disease, curse, or affliction. For some, it is a temporary state. For others, God may have specifically called and set you apart for the joyous life of singlehood. Being unmarried does not mean that you are inferior, insignificant, lacking, or not complete. God calls the vast majority of singles to marry. A select few are chosen for singleness. It is a God-ordained gift. 1 Corinthians 7:8-9 says, *"Now to the unmarried and the widows I say: It is good for them to stay unmarried, as I am. But if they cannot control themselves, they should marry, for it is better to marry than to burn with passion."*

Single, as described by W.E. Vine's Expository Dictionary, indicates that *"singleness of purpose keeps us from the snare of having a double treasure and consequently a divided heart."* In layman's terms, it means that when you marry, your attention is divided, and therefore, you aim to please both God and your spouse. Whether you have never been married, are divorced or widowed, being single in today's society and culture poses many challenges for unmarried Christians. This book was written to help you overcome your challenges as well as provide you with direction, focus and support, and lead you to the journey towards marriage from a biblical perspective. If you never marry, these principles can be employed to help you with your singleness.

Many situations and experiences will be discussed to illustrate the varying circumstances you may find yourself encountering. These experiences are offered so that you may learn from others' mistakes, misconceptions, and failures, as well as for you to gain insight into the course toward marriage. The names of those who graciously shared their stories have been changed to protect their privacy.

In this book you will learn of my life as well as others who were single, living according to God's will and courted with the guidance of accountability couples on our journey toward marriage. It is my hope that this book will lead you from beginning to end in preparing you for a marriage that glorifies God; His will, His way.

At the time of this writing, we have been married for four years. I was single and celibate for five years and Andre was for three years prior to marriage. Although we walked through the process of courtship, there were a lot of things we did not know before we married. This is the motivation for writing this book.

This journey towards marriage will hopefully move you to get rid of all things that may hinder your future marital relationship. The season of autumn, when the leaves -- the old you, fall off, is a time of regeneration in your thinking and choices. The season of spring, a time of new birth, will reveal the fruit of changed behaviors so that you will be prepared when your mate is revealed. ***Be blessed.***

Autumn

Chapter 1

Foundation

■ ■ ■

Grounded in His Word & Getting to Know Yourself

And we know that in all things God works for the good of those who love him, who have been called according to his purpose. For those God foreknew he also predestined to be conformed to the likeness of his Son, that he might be the firstborn among many brothers. And those he predestined, he also called; those he called, he also justified; those he justified, he also glorified.
~ Romans 8:28-30

No longer do the days exist where people marry at young ages. Due to the change in culture and preoccupation with getting ahead and becoming successful, many are delaying it well into their thirties, even forties. Some don't wish to walk down the aisle at all because of the demands marriage and family may have on their time and money. In our self-centered culture, even Christians have fallen into believing the struggles of the marital relationship are not worth the effort. Some men don't have to wed because the one they are with is giving them the benefits of it for free; without a ring, wedding certificate or approval from God. Most of us do not have examples of a godly marital bond from which to imitate. We look at disastrous marriages or cohabitating couples then make an inner vow that we won't live like that. Some end up losing the desire to say "I do" at the altar. 1 Corinthians 7:2 says, *"But since there is so much immorality, each man should have his own wife, and each woman her own husband."*

Broken in Spirit

A few years back when I was young in my walk with Christ, I heard an awesome message preached that still reverberates in my spirit today. I don't remember much of the sermon, but what still sits in my spirit is that you can make it in this single walk, however broken in spirit you may be. People and circumstances of your past may have caused deep hurt. You may be unsuccessful in maintaining healthy dating relationships and wonder why they don't precede to marriage. You may want to get married now, but you are in search of teachings that will help you make wise decisions. Whatever the reason for selecting this book and reading it, let's take this journey to mend the pieces of your spirit and become whole in Christ before you become a husband or wife.

Firm Foundation

You are at a unique time in your life where you have the greatest opportunity to have undisturbed fellowship and communion with Him. Your relationship with God will be greatly enhanced if you take advantage of this season and relish the moments of solitude, building a crucial dialogue with your Father in Heaven, one that will carry you through all eternity. Philippians 1:6 says, *"...being confident of this, that he who began a good work in you will carry it on to completion until the day of Christ Jesus."*

One thing I noticed when I got married was that I missed uninterrupted time. Oftentimes when in prayer, reading, studying or just being still, I would hear my name being called from downstairs as my husband either needed something or wanted me to keep him company. My attention was divided between my husband and my relationship with God. Developing an intimate relationship with Him now will allow you to make it through the times later when family duties call and you are unable to get into His presence when you want to.

The first area that we should examine is our connection with God. Examine yourself to determine what type of relationship you share with our Lord and your spiritual maturity level. One way to do this is to pray and ask God to show you the condition of your heart. Another way is to ask someone that is close to you and more mature to evaluate your spiritual life. There is always room for growth. You may find that there are some areas where you lack maturity.

As it states in 1 Corinthians 7:32-35, *"I would like you to be free from concern. An unmarried man is concerned about the Lord's affairs – how he can please the Lord. But a married man is concerned about the affairs of this world – how he can please his wife – and his interests are divided. An unmarried woman or virgin is concerned about the Lord's affairs: Her aim is to be devoted to the Lord in both body and spirit. But a married woman is concerned about the affairs of this world – how she can please her husband. I am saying this for your own good, not to restrict you, but that you may live in a right way in undivided devotion to the Lord."*

As a single person, you should be concerned with or focused on the things of God and His matters. This is the season to spend a great deal of time really getting to know God, His word and His principals. The relationship, knowledge and heart change will help you to grow and strengthen you when the wearisome times arise. Study the Basic Instruction Before Leaving Earth (BIBLE). Every word will teach you about His ways, His commandments, what He expects of you, all the while developing your character and drawing you closer to Him.

The Beast of Low Self-Esteem

For many years I never thought I was good enough. Throughout my life I had people correcting me, criticizing me, trying to change me into their image. I was more of a tomboy, yet family wanted me in a dress. At that time in my life, I hated them. When I was young I was pretty much forced to wear certain types of clothing around certain types of people. I had to dress like a "young lady." When you are not the one buying the clothes and the adults around you are too preoccupied with themselves and what others would think of them, you end up inheriting their dysfunctions and believing their falsehoods.

My dreams and goals were questioned too. Even as I grew older, I discovered exactly what I wanted to do as a career. I was told it was not lucrative or prestigious and that I should try something else. That something else was the same career the rest of my extended family chose to go into. I actually tried it for a year immediately after college. It was not a good experience; in fact, it solidified my decision not to follow the same path.

Even those that were close often criticized me. If my hair, clothes or shoes were not right in their eyes, somehow I was lead to believe that I was not right. I was not accepted as God created me. High school was a nightmare. Just because I did not wear the latest and most expensive fashions, from top to bottom, my classmates talked about me. My parents did the right thing by concentrating on the basic necessities like a home, food and a place to lay my head instead of going broke trying to keep me and my siblings dressed up everyday.

I believe the worst part of it all is the fact that I have an identical twin sister. We were always compared to each other. Her grades were better, she was the better athlete, she was taller, and she was outgoing and friendly. Everything that was different about us was pointed out and I was the one seen as the "worst" one. This crushed me. This turned me to actually fight against my sister. As a result, I did not talk to her for three solid weeks while in college. It was stupid. She had nothing to do with the opinions of others, yet I unleashed my anger out on her.

Out of those circumstances I developed low self-esteem and became overly critical of myself and others. In order not to feel bad about myself, I learned to become what others wanted. I accepted their flawed perspective of who I was. On the flip side, I inherently beat myself up for making mistakes. I became a perfectionist so that I wouldn't look bad to others as well as to myself. I later learned that when people criticize you they have their own self-esteem issues. When others disparage you, they, in fact, are attempting to make themselves feel better or look better than someone else by placing you under them. I did this too. When I felt that I was doing or looking better then someone else, I felt superior.

No more! No longer should you allow someone's words to have power in your life. Be it criticisms or praise, do not accept them. As Jesus stated in John 5:44, *"How can you believe if you accept praise from one another, yet make no effort to obtain the praise that comes from the only God?"* The Jews of that time were more concerned with the words of man instead of God. We must be more concerned about the judgment of God rather than man.

If you too struggle with self-esteem issues due to the disapproving scrutiny of others, accept the lies no more. You should no longer tolerate anyone dictating who you are and what you should be. God set the standard and no one is above Him. He created you, as beautiful and handsome as you are. He gave you gifts and talents. He made you in His likeness. Now who can beat that? No one. Speak the truth to yourself. Philippians 4:8 says, *"Finally, brothers, whatever is true, whatever is noble, whatever is right, whatever is pure, whatever is lovely, whatever is admirable – if anything is excellent or praiseworthy – think about such things."* This scripture helped me to deal with the words of others. Whenever something was said that was negative and false about me, I would think of true, noble, right, pure, lovely and admirable things about myself to keep the words from sinking into my inner spirit. Get to a place where the opinions of man no longer shake you. You can have success in this area by praying and making a conscious effort to transform your mindset. If the judgment does not line up with the word of God, toss it out.

No longer should you allow anyone to tear you down. Pull your self-worth and identity from the pocket of others. Their opinions, notions that are rooted on inadequate evidence and cannot be proven as valid, do not matter. You do not have to go into battle mode to prove yourself to others. Be who you are. Allow others to deal with their own insecurities and do not give their words power over you. Correct those that are wrong, especially the ones who are in a habit of ripping you apart. If they reject you because of the new you, it is their loss and not yours. You gain emotional stability and freedom and they lose power over your life.

If you do not deal with any self-esteem issues in your life, it will have an effect on who you accept to be your life partner. You may end up tolerating mediocre instead of the best that God has for you for the reason that you do not believe that you are worthy of God's best. You are his best and accept nothing less! Genesis 1:31 says, *"God saw all that he had made, and it was very good."* I underlined very good so that you would recognize the magnitude of this scripture. God created you in His likeness and we all know that God is an awesome God and so are you.

We should have self-assurance in Christ. We are justified by God's grace through the salvation given to us by Jesus Christ, not by what we do or own. Our level of education, career, finances, beauty, status or intellect has no bearing on who we are. Therefore, walk with your head up knowing full well that you are good just because God said so.

Know Who You are in Christ

Being single does not mean you are not a person of value. Reflect and meditate on the following scriptures and see that you are worthy in His eyes:

Genesis 9:6	You are made in the image of God
Psalm 139:14	You are fearfully and wonderfully made
Matthew 5:14	You are the light of the world
John 1:12 - 15	You are a child of God, born of God
John 15:16	You are chosen and appointed by God
Romans 5:1	You have been justified through faith
Romans 8:14	You who are led by the Spirit are sons of God
Ephesians 2:10	You are God's workmanship, created to do good works

When you become discouraged, lonely or doubtful, review God's promises revealed through His word sited below to help you to make it through and overcome your feelings.

Know therefore that the Lord your God is God; he is the faithful God, keeping his covenant of love to a thousand generations of those who love him and keep his commands. ~ Deuteronomy 7:9

In him we were also chosen, having been predestined according to the plan of him who works out everything in conformity with the purpose of his will, in order that we, who were the first to hope in Christ, might be for the praise of his glory. ~ Ephesians 1:11-12

Come to me, all you who are weary and burdened, and I will give you rest. Take my yoke upon you and learn from me, for I am gentle and humble in heart, and you will find rest for your souls. For my yoke is easy and my burden is light. ~ Matthew 11:28-30

And we know that in all things God works for the good of those who love him, who have been called according to his purpose. ~ Romans 8:28

God is our refuge and strength, an ever-present help in trouble. ~ Psalm 46:1

The Walk

Take this uninterrupted time to work on your integrity, develop and walk-in Christ-like characteristics, become dependent on God, trust in His word, build faith, sharpen discernment skills, acquire wisdom, evolve into a compassionate person, learn to love, practice extending grace, hear the true voice of the Holy Spirit, listen to and obey the prompting of the Holy Spirit, and seek God in all your ways that you might be successful. Philippians 2:1-5 says, *"If you have any encouragement from being united with Christ, if any comfort from his love, if any fellowship with the Spirit, if any tenderness and compassion, then make my joy complete by being like-minded, having the same love, being one in spirit and purpose. Do nothing out of selfish ambition or vain conceit, but in humility consider others better than yourselves. Each of you should look not only to your own interests, but also to the interest of others. Your attitude should be the same as that of Christ Jesus:..."*

Research, meditate and grow to be familiar with the truth so that when issues arise pertaining to false doctrine or debatable matters, you will have something to stand firm on. Ephesians 4:14 says, *"Then we will no longer be infants, tossed back and forth by the waves, and blown here and there by every wind of teaching and by the cunning and craftiness of men in their deceitful scheming."* As for some discontent singles, it is easy to fall prey to someone telling them that their mate is coming and all they have to do is either increase their giving beyond what God has already told them or that they have to do an insane act to get God to come through for them. Family and friends, oftentimes with good intentions, can lead you astray. It is essential to stay grounded in God to take hold of your anxiety in this area.

Be careful not to fall for the false hope. Believe me when I say, it is worth the wait when God orchestrates your marriage.

During this season of singleness, you may also want to spend time working in a ministry, developing relationships, babysitting, mentoring others, or serving in the capacity of your spiritual gifts. These activities may help keep you from being idle. Instead of fretting about your single self, you should become focused on the things of God to advance His kingdom. Other things to do include furthering your education, advancing in your career, acquiring hobbies, building lasting relationships or accomplishing some of the goals you have set for yourself.

You also may want to concentrate on learning who you really are, not the ideal you. Find out what causes you to tick, those things about you that may reveal to you the reason you do the things that you do. Get to know your unique qualities and how they can be applied to help yourself and others. There are several books to read including *The Spirit Controlled Temperament* by Tim LeHaye. This book examines the four primary temperaments and the strengths and weaknesses of each one and how they can be changed to be more in line with Christ-like characteristics. Subconsciously, our behavior is directly influenced by our inherited qualities; leading us to become either shy or outgoing. Below are traits that describe each temperament:

- **Choleric**: born leader, optimistic, determined, independent, strong-willed, unsympathetic, hot-tempered, impatient, decisive
- **Melancholy**: dependable, analytical, sacrificial, perfectionist, introvert, moody, critical, self-centered.
- **Phlegmatic**: reliable, calm, unexcited, easygoing, steady, dry humor, unmoved, timid, quiet, indecisive, critical
- **Sanguine**: fun-loving, extrovert, life of the party, forgetful, unfocused, emotionally unbalanced, weak-willed

Another book is the *New Birth Order Book: Why Your Are The Way You Are* by Dr. Kevin Leman. This book illustrated how your birth order may affect the way you behave and how it shapes you. In addition, *What Makes You Tick, What Ticks You Off by* Dr. Mels Carbonell will help you to discover your spiritual gifts as it relates to your temperament. Moreover, there are several assessments you can take to find out who you are. They include the FIRO-B theory and the Myers-Briggs Type Indicator (MBTI).

Once you determine who you are and why you operate as you do, the state of singleness may be the opportune time to deal with any weaknesses that may hinder your relationship with God and others and build upon your strengths to help advance God's work here on this earth. Your weaknesses can also be used for the benefit others, so do not despise them.

In addition, the season of singleness is a time to discover and deal with past hurts, low self-esteem, fears of rejection, fears of failure, guilt, shame, passivity, destructive meditations, abandonment issues, pride, selfish ambition, poor relationships, anger, bitterness, critical thoughts and speech, lying, idolatry, gracelessness, and a host of other issues and dysfunctions that should be healed or spiritual growth has taken place prior to marriage. You may wish to study these issues or seek Christian counseling from a trained provider. If you have suffered at the hands of another through physical abuse and/or sexual abuse, forgiveness may help to bring healing and prevent the past from destroying your future. However, I strongly urge you to seek professional counseling to work through the pains, resentment and bitterness and become delivered from the demonic thoughts and reminders that may haunt you.

Going Through: Managing the Blues

God has given you the desire to marry, however, there are times in this single walk where you will become discouraged being single. Certain thoughts or events may trigger those feelings of discontentment. You may think, *"Always a bridesmaid/groomsman, never a bride/groom."* Any event or program that relates to marriage, courting couples or families may trigger those feelings. Romantic movies, television programs, music or even a moonlit sky may set you up to go through emotional upheaval.

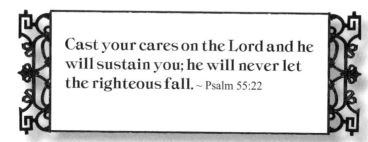

Cast your cares on the Lord and he will sustain you; he will never let the righteous fall. ~ Psalm 55:22

A friend called me to vent. She was upset about being single and wanted to move ahead of God. She also wanted an answer from God. She proceeded to tell me about a conversation she had with her six year old niece. The little girl said, *"Aunt Alexandra, when are you getting married?"* Alexandra asked her why she wanted to know. Her niece then said, *"Because I never see you with a man."* Then Alexandra told her to pray for her. Her niece responded that she did. Alexandra, being sneaky, asked the little girl if God gave her an answer. The little girl said yes. Alexandra asked, *"What did he say."* She replied, *"Maybe."*

I hope you got a chuckle out of the exchange as I did. God may not reveal to you when your mate is coming and who he might be. I believe that if you knew ahead of time you would most likely rush the process and miss what God is doing in you and through you. Be patient.

I shared with my friend that by waiting, she would later see the value of a husband. Usually, when we wait or work hard for something, we treasure it more than if it was given to us. I also informed her of a pattern often seen when women chase after men. The man usually views the relationship as something to be taken lightly, believing that since the woman so desperately wanted him that he could get away with anything because she will not dissolve the relationship. When a man goes after what he wants and what God has shown him, he is more apt to work hard to woo and keep her. He will treasure her as a gift and therefore honor what God has done by treating her as he should.

Well, there is a way to overcome the blues. First, be still before God. There are times you need to stop fellowshipping with the thoughts and just praise God for who He is and what He has already done for you. When you change your perspective you will not focus on the so-called bad reasons for not yet being married but on the good that God has done. Habakkuk 3:17 says, *"Though the fig tree does not bud and there are no grapes on the vines, though the olive crop fails and the field produce no food, though there are no sheep in the pen and no cattle in the stalls,"* In other words, though there is no one in your life at this time and there are no prospects nearby, though previous relationships have failed and you have nothing to show for it, though your hope may be fading and you are weary from the wait. Verse 18-19 says, *"...yet I will rejoice in the Lord, I will be joyful in God my Savior. The Sovereign Lord is my strength; he makes my feet like the feet of a deer, he enables me to go on the heights."*

When you are saddened, dismayed or just plain angry about your circumstances, cease complaining and grumbling to God and others about your plight. Rejoice in the Lord. Even though you do not understand what He is doing, you are doubtful and apprehensive and you see everyone else around you in relationships, rejoice...celebrate...cheer...exult...express joy...be glad and be delighted. Because the Lord is your strength He will enable you to make it through. Keep leaning on Him. Make the choice to revel in Him instead of participating in your own pity party. Your joy will be restored. The darkness of loneliness, anger and discontentment will be defeated by your praise!

Begin by thanking Him for all that he has done for you and through you. Change the focus from yourself to the goodness and glory of God. Remember who God is and what He has done. Trust and rest in knowing that God is all knowing, all powerful, all mighty, a God of truth, a God of comfort, a God of grace and mercy. He has done great things through many and for many. He too will do great things for you. God does not change. In believing this, what He has done in the past for you or anyone else, He still can do. His capacity to do all things remains the same. Praise Him by thanking him for:

- His many blessings
- His sovereignty
- His love
- Discipline

- What He has provided
- Your trials
- Guidance
- Understanding

Second, begin praying when the feelings hit. Ask God to comfort you, give you peace in your heart that lets you know that He has your best interest at heart and help you to continue to press through and stand with Him in your single state. God will hear your cry. Pray for:

- His perfect will to be done
- For your heart to line up with His will
- Peace in the midst of the storm
- Patience to wait on Him
- Comfort for your aching soul
- Perseverance to stand
- Courage to stay the course
- Wisdom to make it through

In addition, lean on God's word and His truth to set you free from those feelings. When those negative thoughts come, quickly take them captive. Speak truth. Meditation on the following scriptures should help you to fight the warfare within your mind:

The Lord God said, "It is not good for the man to be alone. I will make a helper suitable for him." ~ Genesis 2:18

Unless God has specifically told you that marriage is not in His plan for your life, trust in Him, continue to do His will, and do not lose hope.

The weapons we fight with are not the weapons of the world. On the contrary, they have divine power to demolish strongholds. We demolish arguments and every pretension that sets itself up against the knowledge of God, and we take captive every thought to make it obedient to Christ. And we will be ready to punish every act of disobedience, once your obedience is complete. ~ 2 Corinthians 10:4-6

God has given you the power to overcome the thoughts. When they hit, compare them against the truth that you already know. Make those lies that you discover line up with God's word.

Finally, brothers, whatever is true, whatever is noble, whatever is right, whatever is pure, whatever is lovely, whatever is admirable - if anything is excellent or praiseworthy – think about such things. ~ Philippians 4:8

Examine yourself if you act according to your thoughts of sadness, loneliness and depression. What are your concerns or worries? What thoughts have you been fellowshipping in and believing? Once you dwell in lies long enough you cannot tell the difference from the truth.

God already knows your circumstances and truly wants to bless you; however, it may not be your time to get married. He may be working something out that is in your heart, He may be building or strengthening you for the rigors of married life, or He may have something for you to accomplish beforehand. Only God knows the plans He has for you. If you want the best that God has to offer, wait on Him. Ecclesiastes 3:1 states, *"There is a time for everything, and a season for every activity under heaven."* God is in control and He truly knows when the time is best. Last, after all this, take the focus off yourself. Go out and do something to bless someone else. There are several things you could do. They include:

- Call a friend and meet over a warm drink or a meal
- Relieve a single parent for an afternoon
- Take a teenager to the movies or spend time with them
- Volunteer at your church or at a food donation center

Be wise not to get involved in activities that only fill a void, a momentary distraction to ease the distress, instead of relying on God. Activities such as shopping, eating unhealthy foods alone, watching movies or even getting into platonic relationships with the opposite gender temporarily dull the pain. Those activities do nothing to bless someone else or build your spirit. A pity party with other discontent singles is also something you should not use as a source to make it through either.

Be mindful that you must be able to recognize and accept that should God not do another thing for you, you will be okay and worthy. He has done enough. He sent His only son to die so that we may live free from the wrath that we should have gotten for our sins…past, present and future.

Making Your Request Known

If it is your desire to someday marry, begin now in prayer, making your request known to God. It is important that your prayers are directed towards God's will for your life. Ask Him to embark on preparing you to be a mate. Share with Him your desires for yourself as well as the attributes you would like in a mate. I used to believe that praying for a mate was selfish and wrong, that I should accept anyone that God sent my way. How would God be able to meet my desires if I never tell Him what they are? Yes, He knows my heart, but He also asks of us to tell Him what it is that we would like. Be sure that what you are looking for in a mate lines up with Christ-like characteristics. First, ask that God instill those same characteristics in you, but also develop them in the one that is for you. We think we know what we want, but God knows exactly what we need.

Saying Yes to the Wait or No

Marriage is a gift from God. He is not obligated to give everyone a spouse. With that in mind, you must understand that some of you may marry in your later years or never marry. It may not be in your plan that God has set specifically for you. You will have peace in your life when you come to embrace God's call to wait or the "No" that he may tell you. Yes, for those who have a strong desire to marry it will hurt. Work through those feelings and recognize that God has something in store for you that may be better for your life. Pray and ask that He would lessen the desires or take it away completely and to comfort you because a longing has not been met.

The Grass is Not Greener on the Other Side

We have compared ourselves to others for most of our lives. Society pits us against one another, causing us to believe that if we are not like someone who is deemed attractive, has a title or has money; we are less than they are. Our self worth has been stolen from us via the negative and hurtful comments that people have so ignorantly spoken. Unfortunately, words are spoken to make them feel better about themselves. We too have compared ourselves to others with envy in our hearts.

If you would sit back and think, the woman that seems to have a wonderful marriage on the outside may be living in a dreadful way inside her home. What we do not see is the whole picture. Yes, her husband buys her flowers, takes her out, and bought her a nice car. What you do not see is that those things are an attempt to make up for the beatings she gets at home, the cheating with other women, the controlling atmosphere or the abusive speech. I'm not saying that all marriages are bad. Marriage is an excellent thing, especially when it glorifies God, however, we must be careful not to envy another person's life because we do not know the whole story. God has set a specific plan for you. Right now that may not include marriage. For others that are married, God has included that in their plan. When we begin to compare ourselves to others we should say to ourselves, *"It's none of my business. What God has done in their life does not concern me. He has a specific purpose for me and I will wait for Him to fulfill it."* Hopefully, that will put things in perspective for you. No one is better for marrying or worse for being single. Accept that and don't fall for the lies that are so carelessly spoken.

Why Aren't You Married?

As singles, you are often bombarded with the question you detest most, *"Why aren't you married?"* The question wreaks the implication that somehow you are not good enough for someone else. There are several ways to handle the situation. First, recognize whom you are conversing with. Some ask out of care and concern, genuinely wanting you to be happy. They do not understand that you can be single and happy. Have compassion and respond in a loving yet firm manner explaining that you are okay or if not, inform them that the questions or comments are hurtful. Others may speak foolishly trying to be funny or to lighten things up a bit at your expense. Walk away; don't respond to a fool. Second, think of a gracious response. When I had to deflect the nosiness of others, sometimes I just responded that I was waiting on God. Other times I had curt responses and had to apologize. It really depended on who was asking the question. For your sake and sanity, begin thinking about a response that is not malicious. Out of mercy, find a reply that is warm in manner.

For those folks that ask the question every time they see you, you may want to sit down with them and discuss how their comments actually aggravate you, have grace. Ask them why does your marital status concern them so much and explain to them how that question makes you feel. Sometimes you may have to tell them to mind their business. If the person continues to pry after you have spoken with them, learn to avoid them.

Moreover, some people are simple enough to believe that they can circumvent God by giving you ways to get married. They provide uninvited advice, scripts or formulas telling you to dress to attract, to put yourself in places to be seen, or to carry oneself in a manner to be found. They are trying to get you to manipulate the situation. They tell you stories of how other people were found. Some believe that if they work in a high profile ministry that it would increase their chances of getting found. Others tell you to "claim him or her" in the name of Jesus. Let's be real, you have no claim to anything. God gives and he takes away. God knows when your motives are not pure. Please do not follow this whimsical advice and simply trust in God.

REFLECTIONS

` What areas of your life lack maturity? Emotions, trust, character, sexual integrity, etc.

` How will meditating on and memorizing scripture help you to overcome obstacles and negative thought patterns of low self-esteem, loneliness, fear or discontentment?

` What are you doing with your time? How has it helped or hindered you?

` What relationships do you have to help you? What relationships do you need to end?

` What are your triggers that set off discontentment? How will you deal with them?

` What responses have you come up with to deflect criticism?

Chapter 2

Living in Autumn

■ ■ ■

The Purging Season

Therefore, I urge you, brothers, in view of God's mercy, to offer your bodies as living sacrifices, holy and pleasing to God – this is your spiritual act of worship. Do not conform any longer to the pattern of this world, but be transformed by the renewing of you mind. Then you will be able to test and approve what God's will is – his good, pleasing and perfect will. ~ Romans 12:1-2

Righteous Gender Relations

In the world and sometimes in church, most of us interacted with a person of the opposite sex with a goal in mind of pursuing an intimate relationship. We now have to relate in a new way. This modification entails seeing each other as brothers and sisters in Christ, as co-laborers in the war to restore the relationship between God and his people.

A brother or sister in Christ is a member of your family, God's family. Treat them as such. When I was single and early in my walk with Christ, Dave, one of the young guys at church, rescued me from a situation where a man was trying to hit on me. I did not realize it, but men are easily able to discern the motives of other men. He was being my brother at that moment by protecting me from someone that may have had ill will towards me. Treating someone as a sibling requires that you respect their privacy, personal space and keep your distance emotionally, personally and spiritually. You do not need to know each other's personal dealings or struggles, involvement with others or the church and spiritual relationship with God.

As co-laborers in the fight, as soldiers, and as disciples, we have a task to complete while here on earth. That task is the great commission. Matthew 28:18-20 says, *"Then Jesus came to them and said, "All authority in heaven and on earth has been given to me. Therefore go and make disciples of all nations, baptizing them in the name of the Father and of the Son and of the Holy Spirit, and teaching them to obey everything I have commanded you. And surely I am with you always, to the very end of the age."* Part of our purpose is to fulfill this command to raise up other generations that will submit their lives over to God, obey him and teach others to do the same. In doing this, we work with one another to advance God's kingdom. The work may entail working beside each other in ministries, teaching together or disciplining teens and young children. While we work on the mission, we are keeping focus on the task, not on each other. It is imperative that while working together you are not attempting to take someone off course. Exercise self-control. Developing crushes to the point where you cannot work together endangers the mission. One of you may have to leave, thereby; the ministry may be short-changed in someone's talents, gifts, insight, and/or labor.

Being a friend to your brother or sister does not include attaching yourself to someone expecting to get your inner ache of loneliness met, hopeful that one day they may actually like you and be interested in moving into a courting relationship. Nor does in include seeking flattery so that you know you still got it. That's the old way. Being a true friend is one who will confront in love, not cross emotional and physical boundaries, put others interest ahead of their own, being a servant in meeting needs, work together in ministry and someone to discuss spiritual issues, ministerial work and spiritual guidance without shifting into personal arenas. Your brother or sister is not the one to contact when you are battling with lust, sexual temptation, or yearning for companionship. He or she is not your comforter, confidant, rescuer or source of deliverance. Get in touch with someone whom you are already accountable to of the same gender.

It is fine to have working relationships within the ministry, but I would caution against building a one-on-one relationship with your brother, sister, co-laborer and friend. If this occurs, the boundaries have been crossed and you need to handle the situation in a righteous manner.

Accountability

Accountability is providing someone an explanation of your conduct or behavior; revealing your motives. It is deliberately being answerable to someone, without them having to chase you down for information to help you. Accountability is the key to pressing through the obstacles of singleness. Being held accountable allows someone to come along side of you to listen, encourage, affirm and accept you where you are in your spiritual growth without guilt, condemnation or regret. It also includes someone who will share and be a source of godly wisdom and truth while keeping confidential matters private.

Accountability is acknowledging and confessing what you are considering doing before you carry it out. It is not revealing what you did afterwards. For instance, for those who struggle in the area of lust, calling when thoughts and feelings hit is being accountable. Calling after you have given into the temptation of lust such as pornography, masturbation, physical touch or fornication is telling on yourself -- more so confession of your sin.

Another example includes accountability within a courting relationship. You want to see him, but you are feeling quite good about yourself and you feel a little frisky. Being accountable is sharing with someone what you are feeling and asking that they stick close to you until the event passes. Not being accountable opens up the door for your flesh to be the chief decision-maker in these thorny moments. It may lead you over his house, with your sexiest outfit on, grinning in his face. Hopefully he will be wise and tell you that your behavior will cause him to stumble.

A further case includes you having a crush on someone at church. You want to be noticed, yet you understand that it is not for you to recklessly chase after them. It may not be the right time nor season for you to court. Being accountable is telling someone to observe your behavior when in their presence. If you are noticed doing things to garner their attention, your accountability partner has permission to confront you on your actions. Not being accountable in this situation is dropping hints or flirting and dressing immodestly around them, showing your cleavage or pectorals and then telling once you get the desired response.

Last, being accountable to someone includes you exposing desires to get into contact with old girl/boy friends just to see how they are doing or to apologize for past wrongs. Apologizing for a past wrong committed against someone is a good idea, however, be mindful of your intent. Telling after you have called and opened the door for a worldly relationship is not being accountable.

You have to be bold to be accountable. By this I mean to take a stand to be upright, free from fear of what other's may think, willing to be transparent –be honest with yourself and others, and feel no shame for seeking help, walking in humility and admitting that you need others to make it through. There is no shame in seeking help. Usually it comes in after you have fallen into sin and are convicted by the Holy Spirit. You did not listen or heed the prompting beforehand, so now you are feeling guilty. God will give you warnings and a way out, but if you choose to ignore them, there will be repercussions. Nicholas' accountability helped him to focus on God, especially during the times when he wanted to flow off his feelings. In his transparency, accountability has also helped him to pinpoint areas in his life that needed growth.

Sometimes you must face the truth – you did not call on someone simply because you did not want to. In your rebellion you decided that you were tired of being alone, tired of not being noticed, and wanting to fulfill lustful cravings. You caved in to your flesh. You were determined to do what you wanted to do and you were not going to let anyone stop you. Be real with yourself.

Accountability has helped Niemah, a divorced mother, not to settle when she gets tired of waiting. She has strong convictions and she knows that temporary fulfillment or attention will not give her what she longs for, but that she would just get a short-term fix.

Be accountable to God first. Tell him what you are dealing with. Seek Him for a way out. Allow Him to show you how you became discouraged, felt the pull or what caused you to desire something that you are not ready to have. Sit before Him, be still and stay in His face. When you most feel the urge to do something that will cause a chasm in your relationship with Him and with others, call on Him for the power to overcome.

Second, God has placed people in your life to help you to maintain righteous standard. Call on them too. Brandi, a single and celibate mother, shared that she overcame sexual temptation through relationships with other women that she could be honest with. Accountability has helped her because she did not want to have to go back and say that she has done it again. Her partners have also been able to give her strategies to cope. Even in the midst of a perilous situation, the door is still open to be accountable. It's never too late. When you are on the edge of the bed, half-dressed, but wanting to do the right thing, flee and pick up the phone or drive to a friend's house. You owe no explanations. Just get out!

In choosing an accountability partner, it is wise to select someone who is more spiritually mature than you and of the same gender. This person will be a friend when in dire need, be able to discern distorted thoughts and give you the truth, help you through powerful sexual temptation and urges, and persuade you not to put confidence in or rely on your flesh. You should set up and apply an accountability system that works for you. For instance, at my church there is a saying, *"Let's get ice-cream."* This is the code remark for I'm going through difficult times and need to talk or I'm struggling and need some help. At that time we would actually go out to discuss the matter and get the wisdom needed to make it through the situation.

The most important part of being held accountable is transparency and honesty. No one can help you if you choose only to provide bits and pieces of what you are going through. It is not up to your partner to figure out where you are or the truth of the matter. You should be able to be real in that if you desire help, you must be forthcoming with all the information necessary for someone to provide wise counseling.

You only get out what you put in. *"If one falls down, his friend can help him up. But pity the man who falls and has no one to help him up!"* ~ Ecclesiastes 4:10

Be open. *"He who conceals sin does not prosper, but whoever confesses and renounces them finds mercy."* ~ Proverbs 28:13

Be willing to listen and heed the godly advice given. *"Better is open rebuke than hidden love. Wounds from a friend can be trusted, but an enemy multiplies kisses."* ~ Proverbs 27:5-6 and *"As iron sharpens iron, so one man sharpens another."* ~ Proverbs 27:17

When we are left unaccountable, the end result is doing things that may appear upright to us. In Judges 17:6, *"In those days Israel had no king; everyone did as he saw fit."* When we have no one to oversee us, we tend to lean to our own understanding, following our emotions, instead of the truth we know. A friend in Christ will tell you the truth and lead you towards righteousness. Be sure not to use a friend that is not versed in the ways of the Lord. This person will only lead you astray with worldly wisdom, ultimately leading you towards ruin. 2 Peter 3:17 says, *"Therefore, dear friends, since you already know this, be on your guard so that you may not be carried away by the error of lawless men and fall from your secure position."* The season of sadness, discouragement, and temptations will surely pass. Hang in the fight. Allow God to bring you through victoriously. Be accountable, not only in the area of sexuality, but also in major decisions, ministry work, finances, thoughts, attitudes, relationships, career issues and in your attire.

Modesty

1 Timothy 2:9-10 states, *"I also want women to dress modestly, with decency and propriety, not with braided hair or gold or pearls or expensive clothes, but with good deeds, appropriate for women who profess to worship God."* There is nothing wrong with being feminine in your dress, however when your dress reveals too much of your flesh and is overly flashy, it goes against the godliness we proclaim.

In his article *The Soul of Modesty*, C.J. Mahaney states that modesty originates from the condition of the heart. Your heart reveals your level of self-control and discretion. Dressing flagrantly attempts to draw attention, allure men sexually, parade beauty and stir envy in peers. Immodest dress is also a distraction to your brothers in Christ, unmarried as well as married. It causes them to fight undue mental and spiritual warfare opposing lustful thoughts while attempting to focus on church services or meetings. 1 Corinthians 10:32-33 says, *"Do not cause anyone to stumble, whether Jews, Greeks or the church of God— even as I try to please everybody in every way. For I am not seeking my own good but the good of many, so that they may be saved."* Love your brother in Christ enough to put his interest ahead of your own.

The way you dress identifies your allegiance. Modest dress is God-focused, a form of humility and virtue, whereas the opposite is self-focused. Your dress basically identifies whom you serve. When you walk out of your home, God sees you. Would He be pleased? See yourself in view of God's righteousness. It is funny sometimes when women complain about the type of men they attract. Worldly men are attracted to worldly dress. When you wear indiscriminate clothing, it is a signal, alerting them of your availability.

While some of you may not have the means to update your wardrobe there are some things you can do to improve you outerwear until you are able to revamp your wardrobe. They include wrapping and tying a sweater or jacket around your waist, wearing long shirts to hide your buttocks or wearing a jacket over your clothing. You can also borrow clothing from others who regularly dress modestly. It's always good to donate clothing, however, those clothes that are too revealing or sensual should be thrown into the garbage. Do not cause anyone else to wear inappropriate clothing.

To hold yourself accountable to your dress, you should have someone of integrity help you select clothing that is appropriate and critique what you wear. When it is time to shop for yourself, take God with you. You are dressing in immodest attire when:

- Your midriff is revealed; belly button exposure
- Your underwear or thong (should you even be wearing one) is exposed or panty lines show through your pants/skirt
- Your breast cleavage is exposed too much
- Your shirt, skirt or pant is see-through
- Your bra is revealed (opaque top or not enough coverage)
- Your skirt or shorts reveals too much when you sit down
- When your purse or bag is strapped across your chest, it emphasizes your breast
- Spaghetti straps or halters are not appropriate unless you wear a jacket, sweater or top over it
- Bras are not worn and others can tell
- Your crotch is imprinted on your jeans or shorts
- Glitter or words are written across your chest or butt to accentuate those features
- Jeans are faded only at your crotch or buttocks to call attention

If any of these illustrate the clothing you are wearing -- change the item before you head outside of your home.

Women you are not alone in this area. Men, you also need to be modest in your dress. Women can also be distracted by what you wear too. Tight, fitting, or opaque shirts and tank tee shirts that reveal your pectorals are not appropriate. Undershirts should be worn under dress shirts. We are in the days where most men in casual dress wear sagging pants, often revealing undergarment shorts. This too is not appropriate.

1 Corinthians 6:19-20 says, *"Do you not know that your body is a temple of the Holy Spirit, who is in you, whom you have received from God? You are not your own; you were bought at a price. Therefore honor God with your body."* Another area to address here is the wearing of body ornaments in the form of navel and tongue piercing or tattoos. The only thing these ornaments are good for is to draw attention to oneself. Besides the medical concerns, these types of piercing and tattoos divert attention from God. People are more preoccupied on these items than the Christ that is in you. As for men, even wearing earrings is a distraction. We are called to reverence God with our bodies. Leviticus 19:28 says, *"Do not cut your bodies for the dead or put tattoo marks on yourselves. I am the Lord."* Now, let's not get legalistic. Women wearing modest earrings are not a distraction. Women have been wearing earrings for centuries. Navel and tongue piercing, however, have recently become a worldly fashion statement, including tattoos that are strategically placed at the base of your back, drawing attention to your rear end.

Make-up, perfume, cologne, body glitter, hairstyles, colored hair, and manicured nails are not in themselves bad. However, when done to the extreme it too is a distraction. There is a certain grace that modest make-up and hairstyles reveal about a woman. Slightly enhancing what God has already blessed her with indicates that she is not out to seek attention, but she is simply dressing in a manner that underscores her style without overdoing it. Slight scents are very nice, however, when too much is put on; people smell you long after they leave your side.

When one's main focus is on the glamorous or suave look, spending lots of money on the latest and more outrageous fashions, it indicates that their self-esteem is low and they are looking for attention from others to validate themselves. Even extremely long hair in the form of hair weaves or extensions and flamboyant fingernails are a clue to where one's self-worth is located.

Women, I'll pass on a little secret. Most Christian men are not looking for the best-dressed and most beautiful woman at church. The "glamorous one" reeks of high maintenance. The men end up assuming and some rightly so, that they would have to keep up weekly payments to keep up your appearance. Also, they want to know the look of the authentic you. Men are visual. If they cannot see what they are getting into they are not going to chase after it. They do not want any surprises after the wedding night. They are looking for the woman who is seeking God with all their heart. Rebekah veiled herself when she spotted Isaac (Genesis 24:65). This act indicated to Isaac that she was not married. The women that were "found" at my local church killed the princess in them. They wore modest make-up or none at all, jeans, tee shirts, sneakers and ponytails. They were more focused on the work of God than themselves. The "natural" woman was seen instead of the "manufactured" woman they could have been. This is not to say that you should walk around looking homely or unkempt; spiff up, but allow God's spirit in you to been seen and not the outward appearance.

Remember that by nature, men are visual. Christian men are not looking for women who show their triplets -- the breast, buttock and crotch. No one needs to see your "goodies." Save this for the marriage covenant. You do not want to distract a man from getting to know the real you or cause him to stumble.

Singles Association

You may want to invest your time in a ministry or enter a small group geared towards helping singles be prosperous in this walk. These avenues will help you to build healthy relationships, give you the push and strength you need not to give in to your flesh, provide biblical truth, and help you to overcome the day-to-day struggles that singles often face. You will also be able to receive the proper perspective on being single, how to relate to the opposite gender, and how to effectively operate in your singleness.

Fellowship activities with other singles, of both genders, are other things you could get involved with. These opportunities, however, are not "hook-up" groups. The goal is to learn how to relate with the opposite gender and see them as a brother or sister in Christ. I realize you are all adults, however, lets be real -- flesh is flesh is flesh! Ground rules or boundaries can be established as well as having married couples as chaperons. Accountability is key in making a single events ministry successful.

Discern where you are in your walk when you attend these activities. Those who are immature in their walk or seriously "going-through" may not necessarily be able to handle these events with the opposite gender without experiencing strong emotional or sexual pulls. Spiritual growth may need to take place beforehand. Ask those who you are accountable to tell you if you are ready. Here are ideas for group activities:

Informal bible studies	Hiking
Board games	Paintball
Dance lessons (tap, jazz, salsa, hand)	Community ministry opportunities (feeding homeless, restoring homes of elderly, children's outreach)
Amusement parks	Sightseeing
Art galleries	Card games
Free concerts and dinner	Rollerblading
Horseback riding	Ice skating
Cooking classes	Restaurants
Poetry readings or slams	Mass babysitting for parents at a single location
Plays	Teen Events
Book club readings	Informal question/answer sessions with married couples
Pottery molding and painting sessions	Kayaking or canoeing
Go-cart racing	Museums
Theme parties	Bike riding

Options for men:

- Sporting events
- Golf course games
- Retreats
- Photography classes
- Camping with a group of boys
- Group date night with teenage girls to teach them about godly men

Options for women:

- Nail treatments
- Retreats or sleepovers
- Spa day
- Flower arranging sessions
- Do-it-yourself classes
- Exercise classes
- Antiques browsing
- Salon day with teenage girls
- Tea parties with young girls
- Scrap booking parties

Take this time to enjoy the wonders of God. Be still and know that He is God. He will lead you through all obstacles and give you a way out of those that seem unbearable. Grow in spiritual maturity, build your faith, work in ministry, build close relationships, toughen your inner self to handle trials to come and lead others to Christ. Hang in the fight; it is worth the "weight" in gold. Most importantly wait! Only God know when it is time, but also be prepared for when your mate finally shows up.

Do Not Open the Door

It gets a little lonely sometimes. This feeling causes you to desire company. When this season hits, you may start thinking about old boy/girlfriends and casual acquaintances. You know the ones, the cute guy you used to work with or the woman who lives in the next building. In the beginning you have two alternatives. One is to call someone that you are accountable to and the other is to continue thinking about what you might do.

Slightly opening a door starts with a thought that you do not take captive, it then leads you to act upon it, calling the one that peaks your interest. You enjoy the conversation for a while, and then you realize that you have opened the door half way. You have two other options. One is to hang up and the other is to continue on. Choice two opens the door wider.

The one you are talking with is now excited about being in touch with you. They now want to go out on a date. What will you do? Will you tell them it was a mistake and hang up or will you go along with the plans? Humm, you chose the latter. One date ends up being many. The floodgate has burst. Now you are in a relationship that is totally of the world. What will you do? Will you worship God or honor yourself? The choice is still yours.

REFLECTIONS

↘ How are your relationships with the opposite gender? Do they glorify God or your flesh?

↘ Are you accountable to someone who will speak truth, confront, and help you to overcome? If not, why?

↘ What is the current state of your dress? Do you dress to impress man or God?

↘ Are you involved in a singles fellowship group? If not, start one!

↘ What doors do you need to close?

Chapter 3

Sexual Misconduct

■ ■ ■

Relation-trips!

Therefore do not let sin reign in your mortal body so that you obey its evil desires. Do not offer the parts of your body to sin, as instruments of wickedness, but rather offer yourselves to God, as those who have been brought from death to life; and offer the parts of your body to him as instruments of righteousness. ~ Romans 6:12-13

This chapter may seem harsh, but my love for you is compelling me to speak the truth so that you will no longer suffer and be out of the will of God. Being in sexually driven relationships are not only bad for you but they are harmful to your relationship with God. The predominant reason why fornication is so prevalent among singles is because some of you burn with passion. Instead of marrying to satisfy what's in you, you walk in lust and just go for it without counting the spiritual cost. Romans 6:23 says, *"For the wages of sin is death, but the gift of God is eternal life in Christ Jesus our Lord."*

Soul Ties

You often wonder why it is so hard to break free of unfulfilling and destructive relationships. You have been with someone for years, yet you have not left or you took a long time to leave. You are connected to this person on a level that you cannot explain.

He's so fine. All the women want him, but you have him. You are his queen – *his boo.* He makes you feel good about yourself. He even brings you flowers and chocolates when he hurts you. Sadly, it is only to appease you. He buys you dinner and brings it home, saying he will take you out another time. He says he loves you, however he cheats on you with other women. He has brought them to the bed you share. He disrespects you, calling you demeaning names. Yet you stay with him. You give him everything -- time, money, energy, and body. You say you love him, but deep inside you want to leave. But you cannot leave. He has such a strong pull on your emotions. You feel like you cannot live without him. He tells you how beautiful you are, takes good care of you – he makes you feel like a natural woman. His scent seduces you. His voice lures you. You fall for his lies. He has wonderful dreams and aspirations, but he is waiting for you to finance them. You really believe that he needs you in order to survive. You just cannot let him go.

She is sexy, gorgeous, and glamorous. She walks with an air of sheer confidence. She is strong and independent; able to get anything she wants. She is alluring and secretive. Your boys tell you that you are the man for having won such a prize. She makes you feel like a real man. She affirms you. Telling you how proud she is of you and you how strong you are. You buy her whatever she wants – shoes, clothes, leather coats and purses, and expensive perfumes. You pay her car and rent bills. When she is in bed with you, she gives you the best treatment you have ever had. Yet she is using you. She too has her issues. You have asked for her hand in marriage, but she will not marry you. She does not commit for fear of getting hurt. The men of her past have wounded her. She thinks you are the one for her, yet she will not let you into her world. You are filling the missing pieces of her soul. Despite everything, you stay with her. You cannot get this beautiful woman out of your mind. You will give your all and go through emotional turmoil just to keep her, but she says, *"No, I cannot give you all of me."*

The reason we find it so hard to break out of these relationships is because there is a soul tie. An impulsive and premature level of emotional and physical intimacy creates an ungodly soul tie. You felt that if you left the relationship, a part of you would be missing. As your bodies and minds entangled during worldly relationship, you gave a part of your soul to the other. A part of you has departed and now the other person will carry it with them to subsequent relationships. The same goes for you. It's what we call baggage. All the hurts, mean words and mistreatment have left an imprint and scarred your heart.

You question why you keep attracting the same type of person, again and again. You have not taken action to deal with the pain and issues from previous relationships. You jump from one relationship to another to anesthetize you pain. Unless you stop and face up to the real issues, your own, you will continue in an endless cycle. It is lunacy – doing something over and over again while believing you will get a different outcome. You have an unfulfilled need and by being in relationships, you think that it will be met.

Sexual activity outside of marriage is sin. 1 Corinthians 6:15-16 says, *"Do you not know that your bodies are members of Christ himself? Shall I then take the members of Christ and unite them with a prostitute? Never! Do you not know that he who unites himself with a prostitute is one with her in body? For it is said, 'The two will become one flesh.'"*

When you have sexual relations with someone outside the boundaries of a marriage covenant, transference of spirits takes place from one person to the other. You will receive from that person whatever that person carries in their spirit and soul. You may acquire demonic invasions of despair, low self-esteem, suicidal thoughts, rejection and a host of other baggage that the person carries. Next thing you know you will go through trials in your mind and then attempt to reach a conclusion as to why you feel the way you do and what caused it. So, whatever your sexual partner is plagued with, it knits itself within you and attaches to your soul. This stays with you and affects future relationships.

These soul ties may cause you to build walls of protection, more like fortresses around you heart in any type of relationships, even those where people are trying to help you. These walls safeguard and hide you. The "real" you cannot be seen. You used to show your true self in the past, but after many hurt feelings, you hid. You feel that if you open up, they would not like the "real" you and hurt may resurface, no matter what the person says or does. The protective strategies that you may employ include:

- Being fake, a false facade, acting like you are alright when you are not
- Not exposing hurts, fears, even wants and desires
- Keeping people at a distance
- Not allowing anyone to touch your emotions
- Not telling intimate secrets or exposing what is really going on
- Intentionally leaving out details, giving bits and pieces of information, hoping that the whole story will not be discovered
- Lying or exaggerating about yourself

There are many affects from soul ties. Soul ties may keep you from seeing your mate. Your mind may be so affected and clouded by your past, that when he/she shows up you are oblivious. Soul ties will have you to blame others for the harmful ways of previous mates. When you finally do get married, if not dealt with, your spouse will receive the brunt of the punishment you wanted to give to the one who sinned against you. Soul ties will keep you from trusting. You will not open up or let in your God-ordained mate out of fear that you will get hurt, just like the others have hurt you.

Moreover, during the times when you are weak, your strength and resolve is not intact, memories from previous dalliances can be a trigger to set you on a course that you consciously did not intend to follow. When you see, hear or smell something that reminds you of an old partner, you tend to feel that you are somehow missing something and develop a lust for that past life. You ultimately end up in sin if you choose to respond to the temptation.

Unholy Alliance

1 Thessalonians 4:3-6 says, *"It is God's will that you should be sanctified: that you should avoid sexual immorality; that each of you should learn to control his own body in a way that is holy and honorable, not it passionate lust like the heathen, who do not know God; and that in this matter no one should wrong his brother or take advantage of him. The Lord will punish men for all such sins, as we have already told you and warned you."* If you are in a relationship with the hope that he will someday marry you, recognize that you are only fooling yourself. Why would he marry you if

you already give him everything a wife would? In truth, you are actually prostituting yourself. You are giving away your precious pearls without a commitment to get what you think you need from him. You get affection, self-worth, money, clothes, and nice dinners -- treated real special. He gets sex. You may even be in a relationship where he is financially supporting you and possibly your children. This "sugar daddy" pays your car note, rent and even buys food. You believe you cannot support yourself, so you give him sex so that he can continue to take care of you. You don't realize that he does these things to keep you around for his own self-esteem's sake. And then, you get a ring. But is it an engagement ring or a friendship ring? Appeal to someone to ask him and see what he says of the relationship. There is a price you and your children pay for your disobedience. You end up with a broken spirit and a host of consequences, yearning for him to fill voids that only God can fill.

Common Law Marriage

You are living a lie, believing that you are legally together when you are not because you have been with him for so long. There is no covenant. This is a worldly term to make women feel better about actually being taken for a long ride. It eases the guilty conscious. Oh, so you are engaged. How long has it been? *Seven years?!* Let's be real. Do you honestly believe that you will get married anytime soon? You have persevered through all these years and have nothing to show for it. He has given you a number of excuses, promising you that he will marry you.

Maybe, he claims, the time is not right. Why don't you wait until:

- He completes child support payments -- his youngest is five years old
- He gets a better job -- he has not yet looked in the classifieds
- He gets enough money to buy you a ring -- you are on lay-away
- He gets enough money to pay for the wedding -- the cost for a courthouse ceremony is minimal (have a reception later)
- He wants to buy a house first -- with no savings, the paycheck is spent as soon as he gets it
- He's waiting for the right time -- he needs to know more about

you, what more does he need to know?

• He wants to be a better man for you -- if he has not changed, what makes you think he will?

The excuses are plentiful. You will not leave because you do not want to feel the pain nor do you wish to be alone. Pride often keeps us in relationship that we ought not to be in. Your self-worth is wrapped up in a man. You think you are less than a woman if you cannot keep a man or you are overly concerned with what others may think of you. The thought swirls in your head, "Girl, you let that fine man go! What's your problem?" Oh, please!

There are also some women who are in long-term engagements with men who want to marry them, but they will not because they do not trust them. Why then are they still connected?

Do not be deceived: God cannot be mocked. A man reaps what he sows. The one who sows to please his sinful nature, from that nature will reap destruction; the one who sows to please the Spirit will reap eternal life. ~ Galatians 6:7-8

Are you waiting on a commitment from him? Sometimes it just so happens that while you are waiting around for him, he's out looking for a real wife, right under your nose. He wants a woman that respects herself, one that has standards and takes pride in and honors oneself. She does not need a man to validate herself. She knows where he self-worth lies. You, on the other hand, are dependent, fearful, lack self-esteem and have no reasonable standard. You believe you cannot live without him. You do not trust God. Do not lose you eternal place in heaven for a man.

Now let's flip the script. Are you the one that is paying all the bills, including his student loans and child support payments? Is he drinking all of your milk, eating your food, and putting his slippers on your coffee table? Does he not have a job? He sits around your home all day while you are at work. Sure, he cleans a little, washes clothes, vacuums, and even cooks sometimes. He should be, he's living there for free! You really believe that he is doing something. He tells you, *"Baby, I am going to get it together soon."* But, he never does. He loves you! Give yourself and me a break! No women should be taking care of a man in that manner. He is no longer a child and you are not his mother. A man… a husband, should be taking the position as the head. Not you. Paul says in Ephesians 5:23, *"For the husband is the head of the wife as Christ is the head of the church, his body, of which he is the Savior."* Note the operative word: **husband**.

Oh, he's married. Are you expecting him to drop his wife for you? You are being exploited to fulfill an unmet need; something that may very well be missing in his marriage. However, you are not supposed to be the one to meet that need. I realize it may be hard for you because you are also getting your desires met. He's attentive, listens and satisfies your sexual cravings. Please do not sell yourself short. What can a married man possibly do for you? You are not getting his best, nor are you on his priority list. He is not committed, nor obligated to you in any manner. Hebrews 13: 4 says, *"Marriage should be honored by all, and the marriage bed kept pure, for God will judge the adulterer and all the sexually immoral."* When adultery is committed it is a sin against God in addition to the spouse.

Sweetheart, you are worth more than rubies and gold. When God made you He had a plan for your life. He made no mistakes when he created you. Genesis, 2:20b-24 states, *"But for Adam no suitable helper was found. So the Lord God caused the man to fall into a deep sleep; and while he was sleeping, he took one of the man's ribs and closed up the place with flesh. The Lord God made a woman from the rib he had taken out of the man, and he brought her to the man."* God has made you to be the helpmate of your husband, not your boyfriend. You actually have the power to control the relationship. The ball is in your court. You allowed and accepted the bad behaviors. Now, you can repent and take a stand for righteousness. Say no and do not fall back into allowing a man to run you. He is not your God. Do not fear him. What can he do to you? (Psalm 118:6)

Men, you are not exempt! If God has not shown you that she is your wife, why then are you using her? You should be spending time with God and allowing Him to mold you into the man that He created you to be. Most men who struggle with leaving women alone have serious self-esteem issues. You feel that having a woman on your arm validates you.

You look great with a fine woman hanging on your every word. You are looking to her to fill the emptiness in your soul. Know who you are in Christ and review the scriptures that show you your worth. It's not in a woman.

Some of you men are taking advantage of weak-willed woman and allowing them to take care of you. Who is the weak one here? You cannot take care of anyone else if you have not yet learned to take care of yourself. Stand up! Be the man God has called you to be.

Others of you are holding on to a woman until something better comes along. How selfish is that? You are keeping her from her ordained mate. Would you like it if another man were holding on to yours? For those of you that are confident that she is the one, what more do you need to know about her. You have been with her for years, yet you fail to honor her. Pray and ask God to direct you in this area.

Mock Marriage: Cohabitation

According to Dr. Neil Clark Warren, there are two categories of cohabitation or living together without the covenant of marriage. The first type is living together for the purposes of luxuriating in the benefits. This relationship is focused on such things as companionship, joined income, convenience of sex and collective household responsibilities. There is no plan to build a foundation for a successful marriage. This relationship offers the freedom to leave once the relationship becomes unpleasant or dissatisfying. The second type is an experiment or testing to see if they could relate in a marriage. They falsely believe that if they know what they are getting into beforehand, then maybe they will be able to make it in a long-term marital relationship.

Making a provisional pledge is the footing for the cohabitation relationship. It is a mock marriage. As long as the relationship runs smoothly, you will stick around. However, when things get tough, the tough get going. Selfishness plays a huge part in the relationship. It is self-focused. The prevalent attitude is, *"As long as I am happy and my needs are met, I'll stay."* Some women will go so far as believing that if they treat him well and give their all, surely he will want her for a wife. This form of manipulation does not work.

There is no incentive to work on the relationship. There is no security, freedom to be yourself for fear that the other may not like what they see and withdraw from the relationship, or hope for long-term commitment. Outside of a marital relationship the commitment level is weak. This weakness goes unnoticed until hardships appear; adversity that couples in a healthy marriage face and overcome. The sad part is that once married, the same mind-set is brought into the marital union. This greatly affects the marriage relationship. When times of testing arrive such as communication breakdowns, crisis or tragedy strikes, or financial disagreements or downfall, it is easy for the spouses to depart.

Stumbling Block

2 Corinthians, 6:3 states, *"We put no stumbling block in anyone's path, so that our ministry will not be discredited."* Some of you Christians are sexually active, yet you are supposed to represent what a godly man or woman is supposed to be; your ministry is tarnished and compromised. This is what people mean in part when they complain about Christians being hypocrites; your actions differ from what comes out of your mouth.

How will your brother or sister in Christ ever truly see God if you show them the exact opposite? In Mark 12:30-31, Jesus says, *"Love the Lord your God with all your heart and with all your soul and with all you mind and with all your strength. The second is this: 'Love your neighbor as yourself.' There is no commandment greater than these."* Love your boyfriend or girlfriend enough to care about his or her soul by no longer having them partake in your sin. You know what is righteous in the eyes of the Lord, they may not.

You may very well be blocking what God is trying to do in your life as well as in the life of someone else when you choose to be in worldly relationships. You are setting a poor example. Romans 6:1-18 wholly relates to what I'm trying to convey to you at this point. While reading, keep your mind on the message that God is trying to share with you. I hope you are able to pull something from it to help you.

What shall we say, then? Shall we go on sinning so that grace may increase? By no means! We died to sin; how can we live in it any longer? Or don't you know that all of us who were baptized into Christ Jesus were baptized into his death? We were therefore buried with him through baptism into death in order that, just as Christ was raised from the dead through the glory of the Father, we too may live a new life.

If we have been united with him like this in his death, we will certainly also be united with him in his resurrection. For we know that our old self was crucified with him so that the body of sin might be done away with, that we should no longer be slaves to sin - because anyone who has died has been freed from sin.

Now if we died with Christ, we believe that we will also live with him. For we know that since Christ was raised from the dead, he cannot die again; death no longer has mastery over him. The death he died, he died to sin once for all; but the life he lives, he lives to God.

In the same way, count yourselves dead to sin but alive to God in Christ Jesus. Therefore do not let sin reign in your mortal body so that you obey its evil desires. Do not offer the parts of your body to sin, as instruments of wickedness, but rather offer yourselves to God, as those who have been brought from death to life; and offer the parts of your body to him as instruments of righteousness. For sin shall not be your master, because you are not under law, but under grace.

What then? Shall we sin because we are not under law but under grace? By no means! Don't you know that when you offer yourselves to someone to obey him as slaves, you are slaves to the one whom you obey - whether you are slaves to sin, which leads to death, or to obedience, which leads to righteousness? But thanks be to God that, though you used to be slaves to sin, you wholeheartedly obeyed the form of teaching to which you were entrusted. You have been set free from sin and have become slaves to righteousness.

Women – do not fret. There is a man for you. His name is Jesus Christ. The One you cannot live without. Even in your situation, he loves you and is waiting patiently for you to be dependent on him. He will give you all that you need – unconditional love, acceptance, promises that will not be broken, support, encouragement, comfort and healing. He will fill your voids and meet your daily provisions. He is all the man you need. He will not cheat on you, tell you lies, abuse or betray you. No man can compare to the love of Jesus Christ. He gave his life for you -- a painful death on the cross so that you can live free, sanctified and holy before God. He will give you peace beyond your imagination. He is your advocate. He will plead before God for you! You have an eternal home because of Him. No mere man could give you that.

Men, you say you are in search of a real man, one that will treat you like a son. Look no further. His name is Jesus Christ. He will teach you his ways, strengthen you and love you like no earthly father can. He will show you how to be a true man of God. He will mold you into a patient, kind and loving man. He will hug you like no other. He will comfort you and wipe away your tears of hurt. He will not abandon you. He will be with you always. He will affirm and encourage you. He believes and hopes in you. He has your best interest at heart. He loves you unconditionally. He will never forsake you. He is all the man you need. He prays to God in your behalf that you will have a prosperous life on earth. He will set you on high, allowing you to lead your family. Count it an honor that God chose you to care for his people.

A longing fulfilled is sweet to the soul, but fools detest turning from evil. ~ Proverbs 13:19

If you are in a cohabitation or long-term relationship, in submission to God's principle, move out and break it off. This is not a godly relationship. God may intend for you to get married, but not now. Separately, both of you need time to develop a proper relationship with God and mature in your walk. If it is God's will for you all to be in an ordained marital covenant, He will bring you back together in His time. If He determines that you two will not be brought back together, mourn and move on.

Virginity and Celibacy

For you pure, undefiled virgins -- stay that way until your wedding night! Save love-making for marriage. The thrill of being dethroned is over as soon as the act ends. Sadly enough, giving or taking virginity is a game of conquest. Once conquered you lose your self-respect, reputation, testimony, and dignity and end up with feelings of guilt or shame.

Worldly sex is not what it is cracked up to be. It fills no void; it doesn't give you what you need. All it does is take -- your body, mind and spirit. Just because you have not had intercourse, know that sexual touch and oral stimulation outside the bounds of marriage is considered sexual sin -- it too has consequences. Ephesians 5:3 says, *"But among you there must not be even a hint of sexual immorality, or of any kind of impurity, or of greed, because these are improper for God's holy people."*

For the rest -- most important, rid yourself of all things that are sexual in nature. Fornication, masturbation and pornography are sin. Eliminate all ties with former lovers and pursue celibacy. It is well worth it. This is the most difficult area to master for singles that are and have been sexually active. Celibacy is a choice. Once you make the choice, for some, the desire for sexual relations diminishes immediately, for others it may take some time. In complete surrender and obedience to God, break off any sexual ties and press not to put yourself in tempting situations.

> *"I've recently been in contact with an old boyfriend, just talking about the past issues and mistakes made between the two of us. Months later, the frustration of being single hit and I decided I was going to have sex. I didn't want to play by the Christian rules any longer. I got tired of seeing people not living right and being*

hooked up with a "saved" man and I was still single. I decided to have sex one weekend if my old boyfriend "dropped by." Of course he didn't and the frustration passed. I decided to take off of work that Monday to work on a school paper that was due on Tuesday.

Early Monday morning, I realized that I didn't have a computer so I needed to go to work. I did. About two hours later I received a call from my old boyfriend. He asked where I was and told me he was in front of my house and that he wanted to visit. I was at work. Soon after I got off the phone I said, "God will keep you even when you don't want to be kept." Had he come to visit over the weekend or while I had been home that morning, I probably would have done it or had to fight him off to keep from doing it."
~ Alexandra

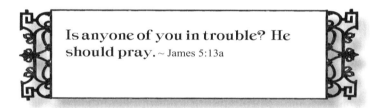

Is anyone of you in trouble? He should pray. ~ James 5:13a

Overcoming the flesh in this area requires prayer, patience and accountability. This seems like a never-ending battle, but with self-control and perseverance you will make it through. You may stumble and fall, but when you do, learn from your mistakes, pick yourself up and keep moving forward.

Nicholas was celibate for two years. But, because of his lack of accountability he relapsed. He advises other men is to get to know God, be accountable, share thoughts with other men, be open to hearing "No," seeing God in the answer and develop relationships with those that are more spiritually mature. Since that time he has been celibate for almost three years. Lauren has also been celibate for two years, but for the same reason she too relapsed. She suggests that you value yourself and your relationship with God enough to remain celibate, stay connected with other godly singles and not to walk it alone. Others have been able to stand for longer periods. Although she still struggles, Brandi has been celibate for over five years. Having accountability partners has been a great help for her in this area.

Over time, the soul-ties will be broken and the power of the memories will fade. Be encouraged and seek help when you need it. Abstinence will purge you of sexual immorality, just be patient, your soul, mind and body will one day be free from the effects of past dalliances.

Deal with any compromises in your life. Exodus 34:12 says, *"Be careful not to make a treaty with those who live in the land where you are going, or they will be a snare among you."* The direction you are headed in does not have room for concessions. You not only will provide a trap for yourself, but also for your future family.

Be on Guard

Sexual temptation is nothing neither new nor unusual. Throughout history, many men and women have fallen into the trap of temptation. Temptation in itself is not wrong, it is actually a test; acting upon sexual temptation is sin. Whenever you decide to do the right thing, the tempter comes in and attempts to take you off your course. However, you are tempted by what is already in your heart. James 1:13-15 says, *"When tempted, no one should say, 'God is tempting me.' For God cannot be tempted by evil, nor does he tempt anyone; but each one is tempted when, by his own evil desire, he is dragged away and enticed. Then, after desire has conceived, it gives birth to sin; and sin, when it is full-grown, gives birth to death."*

Stephen, a divorced father of two, had been in a men's class at his church. The discussion centered on the sin that so easily entangled us. Stephen believed that most men had a problem with lust, except him. He felt that because he had been celibate for over four years, he had lust conquered. He told the group that he was fine and that it was not a weakness in his life. He actually thought that he was better, a super-Christian, because he did not concede to lust; he was in control.

A year later he was on a date at his home. He and his friend were watching a religious program on television. Although they had boundaries in place, she began to coyly look at him. Eventually she jumped on him. They ended up hugging and it progressed to kissing. They had to forcefully push themselves apart. Stephen felt guilty. He felt like a Pharisee. It brought him to his knees. He thought he had overcome lust. His guilt was so strong that he considered hugging and kissing to be sex. He thought all those years of celibacy were in vain. After he got over his failure, he realized that he was not superman and could not succeed in this area on his own. The incident showed him how much he needed God and how much God has kept him. Stephen learned that when God takes His hand off you for a second, your true self would come out.

Always remember that Satan uses those desires that are already in your heart to get you! Work on your heart in those areas that may hinder you. When matured, Satan can no longer attack you in that area. The stronghold has been broken.

There are several other things you could do to protect yourself from being tempted. The first is to be mindful of allowing spiritually unhealthy things into your mind. These include watching television or movies with sexual content, listening to secular love songs, and conversation about sexuality with people who consider physical intimacy as normal in the context of dating relationships and reading romantic novels. When the unhealthy visions and thoughts enter into your mind, redirect your attention elsewhere. Instead of mulling over them and trying to fight it off, think about something else. Change your frame of mind to that which is good.

Second, do not put yourself in alluring situations. These include one-on-one "friendship" dates with the opposite sex just to go out and have fun, visiting opposite gender "friends" at their home to help them out or so-called bible study sessions with someone of the opposite sex. This is a great time to reinforce accountability practices.

Moreover, become familiar with scripture. Even Jesus was tempted. He was wise and strong enough to rely on the truth of God's word to help him to overcome. This is what we must do. God's word is a tool to use and is our way out. Many are available to help you fight the temptations.

Last, continual prayer will help you. Jesus directed us on how we should pray, Matthew 6:13 says, *"And lead us not into temptation, but deliver us from the evil one."* Pray always, even before you are tempted so that you will have the peace and protection of God to overcome it.

Know that you will be tested. Whenever we say we are going to do something, we are tested to see if we will hold to our word. When the state of arousal hits, examine yourself. What do you feel you are missing?

What conversations have you been involved with? What memories may have triggered the feeling? What have you allowed in your spirit? What lustful thoughts have taken you captive? What are you looking to fulfill? For some there is no quick fix, especially when you have been in a sexual relationship for a long time.

Remember, be careful as to what you allow yourself to view or hear. Be mindful that oftentimes when we see, read or listen to some things, it may cause us to develop discontentment in the state of singleness. The television, secular music and magazines, romantic novels, even inappropriate conversations may stir up the old nature, causing us to stumble. DO NOT PUT CONFIDENCE IN YOUR FLESH! (1 Corinthians 10:12). Matthew 26:41 says, *"Watch and pray so that you will not fall into temptation. The spirit is willing, but the body is weak."* Even as a married person, I must be wise in what I allow to infiltrate my spirit, lest I compare and become dissatisfied with my husband.

1 Corinthians 10:13 states, *"No temptation has seized you except what is common to man. And God is faithful; he will not let you be tempted beyond what you can bear. But when you are tempted, he will also provide a way out so that you can stand up under it."* God will open a door for you to flee the situation; however, do not test God, believing that you can handle temptation, when in fact you cannot. Just like children push the limit with their parents just to see what they can get away with, so we as adults try to push our limits with God. The only difference is that parents may not see everything, but God does. He knows what is in your heart and your motives. No one gets away with anything over God, so why try?

Nicolas realized that subtle things like an intimate conversation, an "innocent" joke with sexual overtones and thoughts stored in his head caused sexual temptation in his life. To safeguard his spirit, he now avoids movies with sex scenes and women with their breast hanging out because he acknowledges the high price for feeding his flesh.

What is it Worth?

What is it worth for you to live the life that reflects the very nature of Christ? A life of purity, patience, steadfastness, loyalty to God, a servants heart, obedience, love, clean heart, sane mind, freedom, peace, fellowship, relationships, mentors, disciples, hedge of protection – living for God.

Ask yourself: will living for God cause you to lose more than you gain by doing what you want? Certainly not! Those things are worthless in comparison to what you receive as a child of God, one with an eternal inheritance. Is it not worth it to abstain? Believe me when I tell you, it is worth a life – Christ's life, as a matter of fact – to be all that you can be according to God's plan, purpose and will for your life. You already recognize that God knows what is best for you. It would behoove you to obey His command and it grieves Him not be able to give you what He would like for you to have. His kingdom cannot be advanced when we continue to live a life of sin. He cannot and will not use wickedness to promote goodness.

It is great that we have a Heavenly Father who loves us so much that He has already orchestrated a wonderful life for us. All we have to do is obey and walk in it. We have to walk under His direction, prompting, leadership and guidance. We obey Him and we will live a prosperous life on this earth until He calls us home to be with Him. If we continue to knowingly sin, we lose our inheritance.

It is not worth it to give your best to a man or woman; yet give God second best. What can that man or woman do for you above God? Nothing! Is it worth it to give your body to someone whom you are not married to? Is it worth losing spiritual ground when you have been celibate for quite sometime only to give it up because you are tempted, frustrated and tired of being alone? Is it worth it to live with someone who brings you constant anxiety, pain, disillusionment, and no commitment or security and miss out on the comfort that only God can bring? Is it worth it to replace God with a man or woman to satisfy that inner hunger or desire?

Is it worth it to carry around strongholds from soul ties and memories or anything else you may have picked up during worldly relationships instead of having a mind at rest and a healthy body? Is it worth it to be left alone, with no one to lean on because you choose not to be held accountable? Is it worth it to give up your purity -- virginity -- to someone who is here today but gone tomorrow? Is it worth it to lose your testimony and not be able to help the struggling disciple that comes after you because you still operate in your old ways? Is it worth it to take someone off course because you refuse to take control of your lustful desires? Is it worth it to want to get a man by dressing seductively, ending up with a man with ill desires towards you? Is it worth it to give into the fleeting thought and subsequent feeling and lose the favor of God?

You want respect but you cannot get it because you do not respect yourself or the God that is in you. Yes, God loves you, but he does not like what you do. God has generously given us a free will. We must determine the rationale for making choices and comprehend the consequences, good or bad, that may result. So is it worth it? You tell me.

You Fall, You Lose

So much will be lost when you know the truth, yet you decide to disobey. Oh, you can stop right at the beginning of giving it up; it is your choice. Yes, I understand how hard it is, but out of your love for God and what He has done for you, let His power reign in you at that very moment, so in His will you can overcome, get up and leave.

The physical cost may include a sexually transmitted disease (short-term, long-term, permanent, or deadly), pregnancy or abortion. There are emotional costs as well. They include a broken heart, feelings of intense shame, guilt, anger and bitterness, especially if the relationship does not end in a marriage.

What is potentially destructive is that when a pregnancy occurs, there is no guarantee that the father will stick around. The child that is born may be short-changed from the beginning – financially, spiritually and emotionally. It will be a hard road when you do not have the benefits of a well-balanced, two-parent household. Sure other men can fill in as a pseudo father; however the one the child longs for is their biological father. The emotional results may be fear of rejection, abandonment issues, resentment, anger or bitterness. Should the father choose to stay in the life of the child, but not sustain a healthy relationship with the mother, it brings up other potentially perilous problems for those involved. Whatever the outcome, a loss has taken place.

Last, the spiritual costs are high. Yes, God still loves you, but he is not pleased. God has given us the principal: you reap what you sow. You may not reap the same as what you sowed; but there are consequences to your actions.

Soul Satisfier - Born Out of Obedience

Your spirit is broken. It has been beat down by worldly relationships. You do not understand. Open your heart and allow what I share with you next to get into your spirit. My hope is that it will give you insight and hopefully lead you into breaking the soul tie and relationship cycles, ultimately leading to you a lasting relationship with Christ. Your thinking patterns would have to change. Your standards will have to increase. You will no longer look to any male or female to satisfy needs that only God can meet. This truth should set you free.

God is the source to satisfy your soul. He will give you rest, He is your refuge. He is your provider and protector, He is your fortress. Repent, turn away from your sin and surrender! God can heal you if you let Him. God is the source to satisfy your soul. He is your help. Pray and ask God to help you, deliver you, and set you free in this area. This deliverance will allow you to be in healthy relationships. Give God all that time, love, emotion and money that you once gave to others. He will do the right things with it and by you. Healing in this area takes place when you allow God to purge you through the spiritual growth process. The memories will not go away immediately, but with healing, the stronghold will lose its power over time. Allow God to help you obtain those things you lack and overcome those that hinder you. Christ is all the "One" you need. Let him comfort, encourage, build you up and guide you. In the end you will have a peace like no other, a true understanding of God's love, and be prepared for the one that God may send your way. The cycle will be broken. Victory is yours. All you have to do is surrender, let go of your ways. Permit God to mold you into the image of Christ. It will hurt. Growth and change always brings about pain. As the saying goes, *"No Pain, No Gain."*

If my people, who are called by my name, will humble themselves and pray and seek my face and turn from their wicked ways, then will I hear from heaven and will forgive their sin and will heal their land. ~ 2 Chronicles 7:14

Deuteronomy 6:3 says, *"Hear, O Israel, and be careful to obey so that it may go well with you and that you may increase greatly in a land flowing with milk and honey, just as the Lord, the God of your fathers, promised you."* Obedience is required for you to get a grip on your life and turn the tide of reaping from what you have sown. It is a decision you make out of your love for God, not out of fear from repercussions. God has provided laws and principles in his word to safeguard you if you obey. Disobedience gives birth to negative outcomes. Choose blessings over curses. There are several rewards for obedience. They include:

Favor from God	Healing
Spiritual maturity	Transformation
Authority	Oneness with God
Freedom – no longer bound to sin	Circumcision – a clean heart
Prosperity (in Him)	Vision
Restoration	Clear perspective
Compassion from God	Completeness
Reconciliation	Fulfillment

I've Fallen And I Can Get Up

We all make mistakes by letting our guard down, becoming overtaken by temptation and looking to fill our own void. We falsely believe that sex will temporarily dull the pain and cause us to feel better.

Brandi was not content. She played with negative thoughts for at least a year, wondering about her future husband's whereabouts. She believed that her time had come to be found since she had been at the church for such a long time. What begun as a school function for her daughter ended up being a kissing session with her daughter's father; Keith. As they spent the day together reminiscing over old times and the love they once shared, Brandi let her guard down. She was comfortable with Keith. She felt safe. She got caught up in the moment. As they sat in a parked car, with their daughter asleep in the back, Brandi gave him a mint and then kissed him. She had already made up in her mind that she was going to do so. Because she was the aggressor, the kissing progressed to heavy petting. It even continued as they went into his home. Then Keith asked her what was really going on. He did not understand why and where her behavior was coming from. She squelched him by telling him to shut up. Then, she said out loud, *"I can't believe I'm doing this. I am getting ready to throw away almost six years."* He was stunned. She told him that she had not been with anyone. He responded, *"You still haven't been with anyone."* Brandi later realized that God's grace kept her. She was willing to give away her pearls and for once, Keith did not want them. During the whole encounter, their daughter lay nearby asleep.

When she finally left his home, her first inclination was not to tell anyone. She immediately drove to her friend's house. Her friend did not pass judgment, was understanding and told her that she was not going to sit there depressed. Brandi was told to get up and reminded that she did not have sex. But Brandi felt as if she did because she knew she had no business being there and she was the aggressor. He did not come after her. When she and Keith later discussed the incident, he told her that she was going to have to use some self-control. She was able to move on and catch her thoughts; yet, Brandi understands that if the opportunity comes up she would probably do it again. Because of this, she knows she has to keep her distance from Keith and become accountable regarding her thoughts.

We must be careful not to allow the enemy trick us into believing that we will be harshly judged because of our mistakes. Confess your sins and be free!

After serious self-evaluation, Brandi learned that she was not perfect. She believes that she almost fell with Keith because her 5 plus years of celibacy was her badge of honor. Whenever a discussion about being single came up, the first thing she would declare was her years of making it. Pride was her downfall. She never gave God the glory for keeping her in that area.

After a few weeks she was able to forgive herself, yet she still operated out of anger towards Keith as a tool for protection. God showed her that she has to rely on Him instead of fleeting emotions. God told her that she could not keep using anger as a defense mechanism. He is her protector, her safe keeper and she has to trust him and trust her discernment when it is time to cut the conversation or leave. She now has to learn to have balance and set boundaries in her relationship with Keith -- as her daughter's father only.

There are two questions I hope to answer for you:

1) How do you restore your relationship with God?
2) How do you get up after dishonoring God, your moral values and your body? You've fallen. Here's how you get up:

- **Repent**: acknowledge and confess your sins to God: Tell Him what you did and ask for His forgiveness. Psalm 32:4-5 says, *"For day and night your hand was heavy upon me; my strength was sapped as in the heat of summer. Then I acknowledged my sin to you and did not cover up my iniquity. I said, 'I will confess my transgressions to the Lord' – and you forgave the guilt of my sin."*

- **Forgive Yourself**: some of you made a wrong decision based out of your emotional state and not from a sound mind. Others may have willingly chosen to disobey, because you wanted relief or out of impatience - not wanting to wait on God. Whatever the reason, get up. If you have repented, God has already forgiven you. Hebrews 8:12 says, *"For I will forgive their wickedness and will remember their sins no more."* No longer dwell in something you cannot change. It is done. Accept the facts and move on by doing what is good and pleasing to God. Moreover, Romans 8:1-2 says, *"Therefore, there is now no condemnation for those who are in Christ Jesus, because through Christ Jesus the law of the spirit of life set me free from the law of sin and death."*

- **Learn From Mistakes**: now is the time to search yourself and find out how and why you fell. Once you discover the mistakes and allowances along the way, an alarm should set off, reminding you that you could possibly fall again if you do not reign in what took you off course in the first place. The following questions can be used as a guide to help you:

  - What subtle things did you allow in your spirit?
  - Where did you let down your guard and why?
  - What was the pull that caused you to fall?

- What was your emotional state prior to the fall?
- What void were you trying to fill – loneliness, discontentment, or impatience?
- Were you accountable to your thoughts and actions?
- Where did you open the door?
- Did you assume that you could handle the little things?

- **Confess to another**: I say this so that Satan will not have a foothold on your mind. When we keep secrets, we are bound up trying to protect ourselves, often lying to keep someone from finding out. Once someone knows what is going on with you, they can help you to get back on your feet. You also have someone to pray for you. There is freedom in exposure. James 5:16 says, *"Therefore confess your sins to each other and pray for each other so that you may be healed."*

- **Go and sin no more**: Obey God. I recommend that you also be prayed up. Become accountable. Establish personal boundaries to keep you from falling again and move onward. Philippians 3:13b-14 says, *"But one thing I do: Forgetting what is behind and straining toward what is ahead, I press on toward the goal to win the prize for which God has called me heavenward in Christ Jesus."*

REFLECTIONS

- What soul ties are present and how do they affect you? How will you allow God to purge you in this area?
- Are you currently in a dating (sexual) relationship? Does it glorify self or God? If self, are you willing to let go and allow Jesus to be the One for you?
- What areas tempt you the most? What do you do when tempted?
- What is it worth to you to continue in a sexually driven relationship?
- What consequences do you think you may face if you continue to be disobedient?

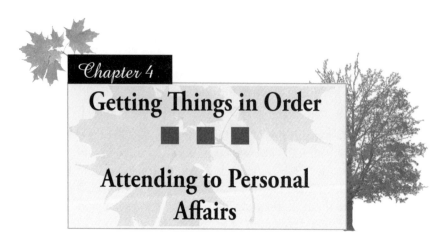

Chapter 4

Getting Things in Order

■ ■ ■

Attending to Personal Affairs

Be sure you know the condition of your flocks, give careful attention to your herds; ~ Proverbs 27:23

This chapter will focus on the affairs that you should address and attend to while you are still single. We are going to tackle three primary areas that if resolved, would place you in a better position for yourself and for your future mate. The areas include developing into a man of God or a woman of character, relationships and finances.

Character Examination

Psalm 26:2-3 says, *"Test me, O Lord, and try me, examine my heart and my mind; for your love is ever before me, and I walk continually in your truth."* If you really want to know what is in your heart, pray and ask God to show you. Ask Him to reveal to you those things that would have a great impact on a marital relationship. The relevant question becomes, would you marry someone just like you? A realistic self-examination should be conducted to determine if your issues will make you ill suited or unprepared for the role of a spouse. Answering some of these questions may provide you with ideas of some of the areas that you should take note of and address. You may be able to develop your own list as God reveals to you those things that may impact your future marriage.

- **What are your pet peeves?** Determine if they are petty, unbiblical and how they may affect someone you may share your life with. Make the adjustment and correct bad behavior now so you do not destroy your future mate.

- **Do you have a need for control?** When you are controlling you limit the freedom of others and place them in bondage, causing them to become a slave to your impulses and demands.

- **Do you have a need to always be right?** Always remember that just because someone does something that is different from you does not mean that they are wrong, it only means that it is different. See the positive side of the difference, who knows, it may end up being a better way of doing things.

- **Are you a hoarder or a spender?** Detecting your tendencies in money management may provide insight as to how it would affect finances in the marriage relationship.

- **Are you vain or do you have high standards?** If you are looking at outward appearances to gauge whether you are okay in the eyes of the world or if your future mate has to look at certain way, you need to find out what God says about you and others and see yourself and them in His eyes and not your own.

- **Does your attitude line up with the fruits of the spirit?** Those of love, joy, peace, patience, kindness, goodness, faithfulness, gentleness and self-control. (Galatians 5:22-23) Or with the acts of a sinful nature: sexual immorality, impurity, debauchery, idolatry, witchcraft, hatred, discord, jealousy, fits of rage, selfish ambition, dissentions, factions, envy, drunkenness, orgies. (Galatians 5:19-21)

- **Are you a perfectionist?** Are your standards so high that you place unrealistic expectations on others? When they are not met do you disassociate yourself from them and count them on a lower level than you?

- **Are you critical?** Do you only view your ways as the only way? Do you pick people apart, always finding something wrong or negative about them in your eyes? Do you ever praise for the good you see? Do you wear people down with your constant criticism?

Becoming a man or woman of God means actively seeking to grow in maturity, conforming to the likeness of Christ, putting old ways behind you, dealing with strongholds, being a servant, participating in ministry, belonging to a church, tithing, studying, reading, and sharing your testimony of God's good news. There are so many areas that I cannot list them all. You have a life's purpose and one of your goals should be to find out what it is. A great resource is *Purpose Driven Life* by Rick Warren. Read it and your outlook on life will completely change.

Unnecessary Relationships

You say he's/she's just a friend. This is the time to sever all ties with old partners and current potentially romantic relationships of the opposite gender. Micah was a god-fearing woman, yet was in a close friendship with a man, trying to have her cake and eat it too. God instructed her to leave Chris alone, having no contact or conversations with him. Although she was not sexually involved, she was getting her soul filled and gratified through her relationship. She finally decided to obey God. Her reason was to honor Him, not the condemnation she would have felt if she kept being disobedient.

For single parents, this is the season to deal with the *"baby momma"* or *"baby daddy"* drama. Be proactive. Sit down with the other parent of your child, letting them first know where you stand and how you would like to work on an amicable resolution to past conflicts and current problems. Together you should set goals to manage child-rearing responsibilities. If the parent is unresponsive and not interested in working out a solution, seek wise counseling before you do anything drastic like keeping the child away from the parent as a form of punishment. This usually backfires in that the child is impacted, not the parent. If the parent becomes hostile, you may need to seek legal guidance.

Another group of people to part associations with are your old worldly friends that have no desire to accept Christ, especially if you have ministered His word to them on several occasions. Develop relationships with those that can help you survive in this wonderful yet tumultuous walk.

Last, build relationships with a married couple with children. Observe how the family is run. This will allow you to keep your focus off yourself while you are helping someone else and also learning what it is like to be in a spiritually healthy family. Find out how to set up a home and what is expected of you.

Emotional Scarring

Most of us grew up in dysfunctional homes; neglected by the very persons that God had placed to care and nurture us. Our childhoods were not perfect. Some of us have experienced physical or verbal abuse at the hands of our parents or guardians. Drug or alcohol abuse along with the behaviors that result have impeded your growth or actually caused you to grow up too fast since you may have had to raise yourself. Others have been molested by a family member, adult friend of the family, or by a neighbor. You may not have had these events occur, but your parents divorced while young or lived in the same house but did not act as if they were married. Others may not know one or both of their parents due to abandonment. Whatever the experience, emotional scarring developed. Your self perception as well as the way you see God may have been altered or destroyed. All of these types of abuses breed co-dependency, anger, shame, lack of boundaries, distrust and relational issues.

Now is the time to deal with the affects it has on you and your spiritual health. Work towards emotional healing and forgiveness so that you do not carry the burden of your pain any longer or bring the results of those dysfunctions into a future marriage. I truly recommend Christian professional counseling. I went through counseling and experienced a great breakthrough in my life. I accepted the fact that those things that happened in my life were not my fault. Counseling has helped me to understand the cause and affect of my dysfunctional behavior patterns.

I have learned how to relate better with people, forgive and not hold a grudge, change my thinking patterns and replace it with the truth, confront offending behaviors, and set boundaries. I also discovered some patterns that were taking place in my family line. I had to disown, disengage and denounce those negative things and behaviors that traveled through my family. By praying and turning over those things to God I can now live free and stop those things from continuing in my own family. There is closure in my life. I wish I did this before I got married because it would have reduced some of the tension that occurred in my marriage during our first few years.

Leeches

In this season of your life, it may be a good idea to move certain people that cause distractions or have harmful impact on your life. You know the ones that drain you mentally, spiritually and financially. All they do is take, take and take – bloodsuckers of your life blood. These people come in many forms. They may come across as an overly pessimistic friend that brings down your mood each time you are with them, causing you to either spend energy unnecessary trying to prop them or their situations up to make them feel better or causing you to join them in their gloom fest.

Others may include the forever down and out family member. They need you to rescue them at every turn. The cousin who refuses to get it together and help herself begs for help – everything is an emergency with her. Other toxic people may include the guilt-throwing family member. You may hear comments such as, "You don't love me" or "If you loved me you would…". Guilt and manipulation are the weapons of choice to get demands met. Others will tell you what another family member has done so that you will feel bad for not doing more than they did. Then of course, there's the co-worker who insists that you help them with each project, but refuse to carry his own weight. He comes in late and leaves early yet you are stuck at work trying to complete the project the he should be doing.

When you see a toxic person coming, your countenance changes immediately because you know that they are getting ready to hit you with another demand for your services. You may want to consider getting rid of or moving away from these "toxic" people. They have a great impact on who you are, your time and your resources.

You know they have an impact on you when the decisions that you need to make for yourself are clouded by their needs and desires. The family members, friends, and church members that always seem to need you for their emergencies - which happen quite frequently. Everything is urgent to them. They want you on their page at all times and criticize you when you will not follow through to help them in their urgent time of need. But when you need them they are no where to be found.

The problem is not them. It's you. You have to take charge of your own life and no longer allow others to run over you. You have to now learn how to say no and stick to it. Matthew 5:37 says, *"Simply let your 'Yes' be 'Yes,' and your 'No,' 'No'; anything beyond this comes from the evil one."* Say yes only when you desire to fulfill a need, but when you feel coerced or compelled to do something, and do it anyway, then you are in sin. Be honest to yourself about what you can or cannot handle. Then tell the person you will not do what you are being asked. You owe no explanations. The leeches in your life need to be pulled out so that you are free from the parasite that can infect your whole being.

Things you could do are:

- Tune out bothersome co-worker
- Change jobs
- Set boundaries
- Use caller ID and not pick up the phone
- Tell them explicitly that you are not able or willing to help at this time or ever if need be
- Limit personal ties
- Limit making unfeasible commitments

Finances - Being a Good Steward

Mismanaged finances are a huge stumbling block to building a functional marriage and one of the principal reasons for divorce. While you are not carrying the debt load of two people, now is the time to properly manage your own finances. The first responsibility you have in the area of your finances is to tithe. Malachi 3:10 states, *"'Bring the whole tithe into the storehouse, that there may be food in my house. Test me in this', says the*

Lord Almighty, 'and see if I will not throw open the floodgates of heaven and pour out so much blessing that you will not have room enough for it.'" Many people struggle in their finances because they do not tithe. The reasons are many, but God tells us to obey Him in this area. We wonder why we are living hand to mouth with financial disaster lurking around the bend. We cannot get some of our needs met because we never make the sacrifice to give. God does not honor those that rob Him. Most of the reasons for disobedience in this area boil down to fear and lack of trust. You do not believe that God can make a miracle happen by stretching His dollars, the money He gave you first. Tithe and watch God work.

The next step in addressing and managing your finances is set financial goals and outline how you will accomplish them.

Subsequently, collect and analyze all bills and debt. Get a copy of your credit report. If your rating is not good and your debts are paid off, contact the creditors and request that they remove the bad rating from your report. It doesn't hurt to ask.

If you find that you are living beyond your means and your debt ratio is not in line with your current salary, I urge you to seek out a financial counselor to help you reign in your spending habits and repair your financial portfolio. This is a good time in your life to set a budget that would get you out of debt and consider saving a set amount each month to cover unexpected costs.

Early into my courting relationship I decided to deal with my finances. I had approximately $5,000 of credit card debt from graduate school and unexpected expenses. I also owned a home and a vehicle. The first thing I did was to limit my spending, stop using my credit card, and pay cash for everything. If I did not have the cash, I did not buy or borrow from someone else to get it. Just before the wedding ceremony, I removed money from my savings plan to pay all but a small portion of a credit card bill. The balance was finally paid in the first month of marriage. I did this so it would not impact my relationship with my husband. I have been told of many testimonies of men and women who had thousands of dollars worth of debt and the problems that ensued once married. I did not wish to go that route. However, if your finances are in total chaos; be forthcoming with the information before you marry as not to cause problems early in the marriage.

However, if you find that your finances are in complete shambles, determine what got you in the bind in the first place. Examine yourself to find if frivolous spending, wanting the latest and most impressive outfit, car, or home put you in a tight financial situation. You may learn that you get your significance from material wealth. To get your finances in order, it may require changing your lifestyle and getting rid of those things you simply cannot afford. You may have to sell your luxury condominium or house and move to a cheaper residence or move in with someone else. You may have to sell your car and buy a "hooptie" from the auction -- one that gets you from point A to point B without the car note. This should free up a great deal of money and lead you to orderly finances. If you are in serious trouble, possibly leaning towards bankruptcy, I would advise that you seek financial counseling from a biblical perspective. In the meantime, you still must deal with the issues that got you in debt in the first place.

Moreover, if you are only making minimum wage or a salary that cannot support a family, it may be time for you to pursue positions that will raise your earnings or expand your education in the form of a college degree to increase your future earning potential.

REFLECTIONS

- What areas in your life need adjustments to bring you in line with God's design for a godly man or woman?
- What relationships do you need to sever or heal? How will you go about accomplishing it?
- Do you tithe? If not, why? What do you lose by not tithing?
- What is the current state of your finances? Do you have a plan and goals set? How does it impact the advancement of God's work?

Blessed is the man who finds wisdom, the man who gains understanding, for she is more profitable than silver and yields better returns than gold. ~ Proverbs 3:13

This chapter focuses on men who believe they are ready to find a wife. My hope is that you will discover your readiness to be a husband and what you should look for in a mate.

Rendered Inoperative

All too often, I have witnessed women that have a head start on men. Women have in mind what they want to do with their lives, are in pursuit of their goals, and are financially stable. Quite a few of them are career oriented and taking great care of themselves; in part, because the men that they have been in contact with did not take care of them. Women have also been taught to be independent, handle their business and not expect a man to do for them. In our community, history lends itself to our men being handicapped, either by society or by the very women who raised them. Society tells them they are nothing while mothers raised compliant men, out of fear that if they stood up for themselves they would be victims of fearful and angry people. This has upset the order that God has established for men. You are strong, hard-working and faithful warriors. You have weathered many storms, overcome numerous obstacles and are now in the process of becoming what God has created you to be. In becoming the man of God, you are now in search of a helpmate. One to come along side you to keep you focused, love you for who you are and build you up to do what God has called you to do.

Momma's Boy

Genesis 2: 24 says, *"For this reason a man will leave his father and mother and be united to his wife, and they will become one flesh."* I realize this may be a touchy area for some men, however, I must write about this area because I have witnessed the affects on a marriage when a man has not broken the ties with his mother and connected with his wife. Some mothers have loved their sons too much by taking care of every need without teaching them how to become self-sufficient or God-dependent. Others depend on their sons for their emotional, physical and financial needs that they failed to sever the bond with an adult son. She expects her man-child to do and be everything for her, especially when a husband is not in the picture. In both circumstances, a marriage can be greatly impacted by the authority and pressure of a co-dependent or controlling mother. Wives usually end up wrestling with the mother-in-law for his attention and care. The wife then feels that she is placed below his mother on the priority list. The mother's mantra is that blood is thicker that water, not understanding the true covenant of a marriage vow.

You know you are a momma's boy when:

- Your mother influences and controls all of your decisions
- You do not share a residence, but she still cooks and launders for you
- You share a residence and she fully supports you financially, even when you have a high-paying job
- You still seek her counsel
- You go to her for financial assistance
- You drop everything to meet her needs

- You still need assurance, comfort and validation from her
- You are very passive or weak-willed, not able to make your own decisions because she has always done it for you
- You have picked up some of her feminine qualities in your actions, speech, thoughts and emotions

If some of these describe you, now is the time to unravel all the influences and become a strong man of God, one that exemplifies the characteristics of Christ. You may need to begin to distance yourself now. I do not mean to completely cut off your mother, what I do mean is that you explain to her how much you allowed her to influence your life and that you need to be your own man -- depending on God instead of her, learning to be independent and responsible for yourself and lessening her reliance on you. In the end you both will be free to live your own life, solely depending on God instead of each other.

In order to help you in this area I suggest that you build relationships with other men to mentor you in this new life. Grow in your relationship with God so that you will be able to discern His voice from that of your mother's.

Mr. Cool

You are the man, confident and bold. You are strong, able to care for yourself without help from anyone. No one can figure you out and you like that. Your strong outer shell protects you against attacks. You are aloof, never allowing anyone to touch your emotions. You keep people at a distance to keep from feeling any pain or rejection. You are hurting, but it is covered up. Your pride keeps you from seeking the aid of others. You heart is so hard, that no one can even get in to love you, not even God. This is comfortable for you. It is safe. It keeps people from affecting you in any way. Most of this stems from childhood suffering. You may have grown up without a father, both parents, or something traumatic has happened to you. Your circumstances were not ideal. You had a rough childhood, growing up without proper guidance, financially stability, direction and most of all true unconditional love.

The reality is you do need someone, God and people He has placed in your life, to help you in this walk. If you are in search of a wife, you cannot be a godly husband if you are not able to let your wife be your helpmate. You will crush her spirit if she is not able to operate in a marriage as God has called her to. Now is the time to humble yourself and allow God to heal your heart. Let Him in first, and then you can open up and allow others to penetrate your heart. It is a wonderful thing when you can walk totally free of your inhibitions, able to feel real emotions, to let go of past events and experience forgiveness. You will be the better man for it.

Align Yourself with God's Will

Proverbs 19:21 states, *"Many are the plans in a man's heart, but it is the Lord's purpose that prevails."* Do you know what God has planned for you? Have you sought Him to find out? Where should your energy and time be focused? Life would be so much easier if you knew what you are supposed to do and why. It will keep your energies focused on one or a few areas.

God has instilled a purpose in each man. He has created a purpose for you and has provided all that you need to accomplish it. Your character, temperament, desires, passions and gifts are geared towards helping you attain the purpose that God has set specifically for you. He will give you all the provisions necessary to achieve what he has called you to do. Your responsibility is to seek him for the vision, direction, guidance and wisdom and then follow what he has shared with you to do. Be in continuous prayer so that you follow His will, not your own, and wait patiently for Him to reveal His intent for your life. In order for His purpose to be fulfilled in and through you, a willing vessel must be available to Him. James 4:15 says, *"Instead, you ought to say, "If it is the Lord's will, we will live and do this or that."*

Men of Valor

A man of valor is one who walks in great courage. This man is brave, bold-spirited, courageous, undaunted, heroic, fearless, resolute, chivalrous, and has nerve. He leans on and trusts that God will bring him through all situations, even those that seem impossible. Abraham, Moses, Job, Noah, David, Paul and Jesus are great examples of men that walked in their position and purpose, following God's instruction to fulfill His purpose for their lives.

Abraham was willing to do the unthinkable out of sheer obedience to God. Genesis 22:1-2 illustrates, *"Some time later God tested Abraham. He said to him, "Abraham!" "Here I am," he replied. Then God said, "Take your son, your only son, Isaac, whom you love, and go to the region of Moriah. Sacrifice him there as a burnt offering on one of the mountains I will tell you about."* God wanted to see if Abraham would be faithful. Abraham proved his faithfulness by obeying and placing his son on the altar. Just as he was about to slash his son an angel called out for him to stop. He told him that he knew that Abraham feared God because he trusted enough to do what God had directed him to do. (Genesis 22)

Exodus illustrates how Moses was used by God to deliver the Israelites from slavery in Egypt and take them to the Promised Land. God spoke directly to him and allowed miracles to take place through him so that the people would come to know that God would bring them through.

Job was an upright man before God. Job 1:1 says, *"In the land of Uz there lived a man whose name was Job. This man was blameless and upright; he feared God and shunned evil."* Even as the destruction of everything he loved and owned was taking place, he stood firm. Although his wife asked if he was still holding on to his integrity and told him to curse God and die, Job responded, *"You are talking like a foolish woman. Shall we accept good from God, and not trouble?"* (Job 2:9-10).

Genesis chapters 6-9 discussed the flood and Noah's story. Genesis, 6:9 says, *"This the account of Noah. Noah was a righteous man, blameless among the people of his time, and he walked with God."* Verse 7:1 states, *"The Lord then said to Noah," "Go into the ark, you and your whole family, because I have found you righteous in this generation."* Because of Noah's honorableness, God saw fit and gave him favor. He made a covenant with him and his descendants to never allow a flood to destroy all life (Genesis 9:15).

1 Samuel 17 illustrates the story of David and Goliath. David went in the name of the Lord to defeat Goliath. He remembered what God had delivered him from and believed that he would do the same. Verse 34-37 states, *"But David said to Saul, 'Your servant has been keeping his father's sheep. When a lion or a bear came and carried off a sheep from the flock, I went after it, struck it and rescued the sheep from its mouth. When it turned on me, I seized it by its hair, struck it and killed it. Your servant has*

killed both the lion and the bear; this uncircumcised Philistine will be like one of them, because he has defied the armies of the living God. The Lord who delivered me from the paw of the lion and the paw of the bear will deliver me from the hand of this Philistine.' Saul said to David, 'Go, and the Lord be with you.'" Verse 45 testifies, *"David said to the Philistine, 'You come against me with sword and spear and javelin, but I come against you in the name of the Lord Almighty, the God of the armies of Israel, whom you have defied.'"* David walked in the strength of God and trusted that He would bring him out a victor in this situation. He did not fear the enemy, but went forth boldly, believing, and won the battle.

Joseph obeyed God and married Mary even though she was not carrying his biological child. Matthew 1:18 – 20 says, *"This is how the birth of Jesus Christ came about: His mother Mary was pledged to be married to Joseph, but before they came together, she was found to be with child through the Holy Spirit. Because Joseph her husband was a righteous man and did not want to expose her to public disgrace, he had in mind to divorce her quietly. But after he had considered this, an angel of the Lord appeared to him in a dream and said, 'Joseph son of David, do not be afraid to take Mary home as your wife, because what is conceived in her is from the Holy Spirit. She will give birth to a son, and you are to give him the name Jesus, because he will save his people from their sins.'"* Joseph heard the angel, trusted and responded accordingly.

Paul was a man, just like us prior to our acceptance of Christ, who was an enemy of Christ. Acts 9:1 states, *"Meanwhile, Saul was still breathing out murderous threats against the Lord's disciples."* In the same chapter, verse 15 illustrates that Saul was chosen as an instrument to carry the Lord's name. Later, he spoke out to prove that Jesus is the Christ. Although he suffered greatly, he persevered to bring the people the message of God's forgiveness.

Jesus was a man that lived for God. He fulfilled the purpose God had set for Him. Out of his obedience, he died a horrible death on the cross for our sake. Jesus was a man who was without sin, pure, upright, spoke out vehemently against sin, forgave, and was used as a vessel to illustrate God's love and forgiveness. He led a life purely devoted to God. Although there is no one that can compare to Christ, we must strive daily to emulate his holiness.

The men illustrated here are great examples of men that responded to the call placed on their lives. Many did not understand why God called them, but out of absolute obedience, they did what God told them to do. These men trusted and truly believed that He was with them and would lead them to accomplish the tasks. And indeed, God was with them at all times, leading, protecting and directing.

A true man of God is one that…

- Loves the Lord
- Seeks, trust and obeys God
- Purposes to become more Christ-like in his character
- Executes his talents and gives for the advancement of God's kingdom
- Walks in his purpose
- Passes down the legacy by teaching and training those he is entrusted to
- Fulfills the great commission
- Perseveres
- Reproduces the compassion, mercy, patience, forgiveness and self-control of Christ
- Stands in the gap for others through intercessory prayer and wise stewardship

Although none were perfect, except Christ, God was able to use them in mighty ways to glorify him. You too can be used in such a way. Allow God to do so by responding to his call and purpose for your life. Intend to be the man that God has called you to be. All you have to do is submit and obey God.

The Man in a Lion's Suit

Remember the cowardly lion in the Wizard of Oz. He was in desperate need of courage. He already possessed it, he just needed to walk in it. So, you too must walk in the courage and boldness that is already inside you. Being passive or timid is sin. 1 Corinthians 16:13 says, *"Be on guard; stand firm in the faith; be men of courage; be strong."* Implement your faith by trusting the guidance of the Holy Spirit to find your wife. Actively pursue instead of sitting back waiting for the right one to jump into your lap. Some men are actually ready and responsible enough to marry right after college or at college-age. Men did not used to wait until their 30's and 40's to get married; they married right after high school. You may find her on the first try or it may take you courting several women to find the "one" for you. Go in with a boldness and assurance that God will direct you in this endeavor.

> **For God did not give us a spirit of timidity, but a spirit of power, of love and of self-discipline.** ~ 2 Timothy 1:7

So, You Want to Be a Husband

What qualifies you to become a husband? Think about it for a moment. As the head of a household, are you ready, able and willing to heed God's will for your life as well as the life of your family? Are you solely dependent on hearing from God for directions? This position is not to be taken lightly. You will be held responsible for the state of your family. God has ordained the man to lead his family under the headship of Christ.

> **He who finds a wife finds what is good and receives favor from the Lorf.**
> ~ Proverbs 18:22

Being a husband requires great sacrifice on your part. Are you prepared to set aside your ways and ideas concerning marriage and learn God's way? Have you studied to learn the role of a husband, one that leads the family in a godly direction and provide, support and train children in the ways of the Lord? Does your understanding of a husband line up with God's view? As a husband it is imperative that you hear and obey the guidance of the Holy Spirit. Are you a man that still has a rebellious spirit, always doing your own thing in spite of available wisdom? Check those that apply to your current character:

- Deceitful
- Idle
- Arrogant
- Pushy
- Rebellious
- Controlling
- Low self-esteem
- Prideful
- Critical/judgmental
- Lack self-control
- Self-centered
- Lack accountability
- Negligent
- Passive-aggressive
- Dishonest
- Abusive
- Argumentative

Ponder and consider the following questions in view of the ungodly characteristics noted above:

- What areas do you need to work on before you become a husband?
- If you do not deal with those areas, how do you believe your family will be affected?
- How would maturing in those areas beforehand bless your family?

Once you have discovered those problem areas, set a plan to work on them. Things you could do include searching and meditating on scriptures that relate to that area, hold yourself accountable to a growth track, finding out what triggers those behaviors and learn how to counteract it with alternative conduct, and pray and ask God to prune you.

Nicholas knew he wanted to someday be married, but he had some areas that he really needed to rid himself of before he approached someone. His efforts were focused on the following areas:

- Transforming his critical, perfectionist and demanding personality
- Accepting the differences in others, especially those he deemed as weak
- Learning to be quick to listen instead of quick to speak
- Erasing debt
- Becoming capable of being vulnerable, humble and accepting criticism
- Exchanging old views passed on by his mother and the world of

what a wife or husband is to be with the truth

The following questions should help you to see additional areas that should be addressed:

- How important to you is your relationship with God?
- Are you able to hear clearly from God, discerning your fleshy motives from his direct will?
- Are you able to receive correction and make the adjustment as necessary?
- Are you willing to submit to authorities in your life?
- Are you approachable, can anyone freely come to you without fear of reproach?
- Are you able to accept counsel from women?
- Are you able to apologize and accept responsibility for your actions?
- Are you able to give praise, support and encourage others?
- Do you believe that as a man you are in control of everything; making all decisions and having the final word?
- Are you financially prepared for the responsibilities of marriage?

The reason I ask these questions is because you are under God's authority, submissive to his instruction and direction in leading your family. If you are not in right relationship with Him or willing to obey, you are not ready to become a husband.

Now Laban had two daughters; the name of the older was Leah, and the name of the younger was Rachel. Leah had weak eyes, but Rachel was lovely in form, and beautiful. Jacob was in love with Rachel and said, "I'll work for you seven years in return for your younger daughter Rachel." Laban said, "It's better that I give her to you than to some other man. Stay here with me." So Jacob served seven years to get Rachel, but they seemed like only a few days to him because of his love for her. ~ Genesis 29:16-20

Last, have you studied the nuances of women -- how to relate, discern emotions from reality, understand disposition and emotional condition, and temper responses or girdle your tongue based upon your mate's mood. This is what you will be dealing with as a husband. If you become aware now, you will understand what is going on later and be able to respond appropriately. Being proactive in this area is paramount to achieving a successful marital relationship. Jacob was a man that worked hard to get his wife. He worked seven years. In the spirit, you must take the time and make the effort to get prepared to become a husband.

Be Still and Know - Is She "The One?"

How do you know that she is "the one?" Many men use the world's value system to determine who the best one to marry is. The world says that the one who is beautiful, has long hair, nice curves - a body built for childbearing – one that can knock a strong man to his knees – a brick house is the one. That quality is not one that will advance God's kingdom in your marriage. Men also tend to look towards the one that has a good job, one that will help support the lifestyle you wish to lead. Men are looking at the outer beauty, forgetting that as the outer fades, you are still left with the inner self. Is the inner-self of a woman pleasing to God? Seek God and find out. Be still before Him, asking Him to make His will known to you. Proverbs 31:30 says, *"Charm is deceptive, and beauty is fleeting; but a woman who fears the Lord is to be praised."*

Raising the Bar

Men, while in search of a wife you should already know where you are headed, those things you would like to accomplish and what you need to get there. You need to determine what type of women will best suit you in light of God's view of a wife. You must not look to your old ways of thinking -- the most attractive women you could find, the one that seems to have it all together, one that will bow to your every command. The new way of thinking requires you to study and find out what constitutes a good wife and will she fit in the plan that God has for you. You must raise the bar of what is acceptable. You know what you value, what is important and what you may need to succeed. Discern if she can stand in the gap for you when you are down and out. Can she pray for you? Will she be able to carry the load while you are away from home? Ask God to be with you and lead you in the pursuit of the best wife created specifically for you. She is to be your helper.

You do not want a woman who is an "arm-piece," one that just looks great; she may not have your best interest at heart. You must do the work to find out who she is. Check in with those that she is accountable to. Find out if she has the qualities of a virtuous woman. Let me introduce you to four types of women you may wish to avoid.

I'm positive that you do not want a woman that flows as the princess. This type of woman expects you to do all the work, meeting her every need and whim, gratifying her desires, yet she does nothing to help you to become the man God has called you to be. She is so selfish that you will go without basic needs. She will not cook, clean nor meet your physical needs. Basically, instead of living for God you'll end up living for her.

You may not want the drama queen either -- one that will go berserk or throw a fit at any moment, inflate miniscule issues, and be led completely by her emotions. This one is hard to manage. Your every word and action will be suspect to judgment. She will expect you to validate her constantly. She is quite needy. She will not make any decisions on her own. She will frequently cause dissention in the home. She will expect you to be on her page at all times. She will expect you to do the spiritual work – instead of reading a book for herself she would want you to read it and then give her all the answers. She lives off of other's revelations. She does nothing for herself.

Jezebel, one who is overcome and influenced by a demonic power, is another type of women to avoid. This one is a nightmare to reckon with. She will manipulate you at every turn to sway circumstances to go her way. She will cause you to stumble and question God. She does not think in a rational manner. She does not want to be held accountable for fear that her schemes will be revealed. The jezebel will come against you and every thing that is godly that you set out to do. This type of woman will lead you to ruin. You will either be broke or emotionally spent.

Last, be wary of the women who sets her sights on you -- the one who always puts herself in your path, seeking to get your attention. Her motives are impure. She is trying to get you to "find" her. Instead of wanting what God wants for her, she is circumventing Him to take control. Instead of trusting God, she only trusts herself. Will this one submit to authority? She is just like an adulteress, seeking to devour. She will attempt to seduce you and make you believe that God put her into your path. She will use whatever tactics she can to get you to be her man.

You Found Her!

So, you think you have found "the one." Answer the following questions?

- Have you brought it to God's attention in prayer?
- Have you asked those who you are accountable to if they believe you are prepared spiritually, financially and emotionally for marriage?
- Are you a man of integrity, able to lead a family under the admonition of God?
- Have you determined your motives? Any selfish desires present?
- Have you concluded why you feel you are ready for marriage?
- Are you willing to be patient during this time?
- Are other single men in your social group dating? If so, has this placed an urging in you to want to do the same?
- Are you pursuing God's plans for your life?
- Are you looking for someone to take care of you?

Next, re-examine yourself to ensure that you are seeking God's will and not your own ungodly desires. Ask yourself the following questions?

- Is she a Christian and walking in God's truth?
- Why her?
- What do you see in her that attracts you?
- Does she fit your profile – cute, petite, great job, owns car or home, no children, etc.?
- Are others checking her out and you want to get to her before they do?
- Does she carry herself to your liking?

> **All a man's ways seem innocent to him, but motives are weighed by the Lord.**
> ~ Proverbs 16:2

Once God reveals to you that you are ready to seek out a marriage partner, if you are not quite sure who she is, then pray and ask God to direct you in this pursuit. Once you are sure, observe her, discreetly ask others about her and seek out whom she is accountable to. The point of this is to find out if she is spiritually mature and prepared for marriage. While you are watching her, be sure not to cause her to cause any anxiety in her by slyly revealing to her that you are watching her. This may cause her to focus on you and miss what she is to be focusing on at the time. There are several things that you should be watching for to determine if she is prepared for marriage. They include:

- Godly character
- Integrity
- Meekness / humble spirit
- A willingness to submit to authority
- Laziness
- Poor attitude
- Quarrelsome spirit
- Bitterness
- Flirtatious
- Involved in ministry
- Self-control
- Insecurity

Take this time to lay low, removing any distractions from your life so that you may concentrate on the task at hand and not be taken off course. This is a decision that will not only affect your life, but that of your future wife and family. Seek wise counsel from those who are honorable married men. Be mindful of telling other single men what you are doing at this time. It may cause them to prematurely go in search of a wife. Also, hold yourself accountable to your thoughts, dreams, and motives. Read Proverbs 31:10-

31 to discover attributes of a wife of noble character.

Men, study and meet with married men to find out what the role of a husband is to be. As a married man, you will be the head of the household and set the spiritual tone of your family. Read books on marriage, women, and love language. During this time also allow God to work on matters in your heart that may be a hindrance to your marriage if not dealt with now.

Men, I admonish you to stay in God's face for direction in finding a wife. There is a call placed on your life. In order to respond, you need a wife that will help you to fulfill the purpose that God has ordained specifically for you. Remember, no one is perfect, but allow God to reveal the perfect one for you.

REFLECTIONS

- What do you need to do to prepare to be a husband?
- What standards do you have?
- Does what you desire in a women line up with God's view?
- How will your maturity level affect a marriage?
- Do you believe that men are to control their home environment?
- What sacrifices are you willing to make for your future family?
- How does your life parallel to the men of valor?
- Have you received a vision from God and how will you incorporate a family within the vision?
- Do the women you check out exemplify Christ-likeness?

Chapter 6

Women

■ ■ ■

Waiting on His Wings

The wise woman builds her house, but with her own hands the foolish one tears hers down ~
Proverbs 14:1

Waiting on God's wings. This means to patiently wait on Him to satisfy the longing within your heart. To wait is to remain unmoving until something anticipated occurs, to be accessible or in readiness, to be deferred or delayed. Waiting patiently is persevering, being steadfast, enduring delay without objection, animosity or complaint. For most of us, especially those who have been waiting for what seems like eternity, waiting patiently is wearisome. Psalm 37:7a says, *"Be still before the Lord and wait patiently for him;"*

Genesis 2:22 states, *"Then the Lord God made a woman from the rib he had taken out of the man, and he brought her to the man."* I want to stress the point that God will bring you to a man in due time. It is better for you not to aggressively seek after a man. Please women, stay out of their face. Focus your energy towards becoming the women that God has called you to be. It is none of your business to find out his marital status. It is not good for you to scheme to put yourself into strategic locations to be seen, to put out marriage vibes by bending forward to show you wares, to physically touch as you talk with men or flirt through your tone of voice -- trying to work it. It is a form of manipulation and a direct turn off to Godly men. These worldly tactics that have been used to gain attention no longer should be applied.

The men are quite aware of the women who have a habit of trying to be seen. They actually warn each other as to whom they should avoid. Case in point, one man has been at the church for one and a half years. It's amazing how many women have literally hit on him. The have asked him on dates, sent other women to find out if he's married or not, and tried to carry very personal conversations with him. They do not know him from Adam, yet they just like what they physically see and delight in his "spirit." He is married. His wife does not attend the church. Imagine if he struggles with being faithful. Oh, how he could have been taken off course by the actions of many. He could have become prideful and then ended in bed with the many who came after him. Fortunately he has a strong enough relationship with God to stand through it all. Men that are "sold out" or surrendered to God are quite wary of aggressive women.

Allow God to put two imperfect people perfectly together. He will bring you to the man that he has made for you. In a marriage, you then will be well suited for your spouse and he well suited for you. Be encouraged!

My State of Singleness

I accepted Christ shortly after my 31st birthday, the month before I broke up with what was supposed to be my last boyfriend. During the course of my first year of walking with Christ, I continued to casually date, even going so far as kissing; thinking that it was okay because I was not sexually active. Finally, I realized I had to let go of men altogether. It actually was a huge blessing and turned out to be one of the best decisions I ever made. No more waiting by the phone to see if he was going to call. No more struggling to not have sex. No more dealing with guys who were only interested in what my body could offer them. That was my naive thinking at the time. Soon after, I decided I was going to obey and honor God. I allowed Him to fill those things that were missing in my soul; those things that I tried to get filled from being in relationships with men.

Delight yourself in the Lord and he will give you the desires of your heart.
~ Psalm 37:4

I remember the next four years of walking in Christ and being single. In the beginning it was not so bad. I was just learning about God and reveling in my new found relationship with Him. Once I became busy and began working in the usher ministry and attending graduate school, I did not have time to focus on finding a man. In the meantime I was slowly maturing and learning His ways. I began to strengthen my relationship with Christ. I embarked on reading books that gave me wisdom and got in relationships with women who could help me in this walk.

I acquired a roommate a short while later. Oh, what a blessing. I went in the situation with the belief that I was doing my godly duties by helping out a friend. I soon learned that I was more blessed by her being there than she was. My roommate helped me to see my imperfections. I was such a neat freak. When she looked at my home to see if she wanted to move in she told me she was uncomfortable because she did not want to ruin anything. I reassured her that it was alright for her to move in. I soon learned that it no longer mattered if anything was out of order; resulting in me understanding that material possessions were not that important in comparison to the value of people and relationships.

During our three years together I learned more of who I was and how I operated. I was somewhat quiet, critical and a perfectionist. Having a melancholy/phlegmatic temperament, I was also quite reserved. She was a sanguine/melancholy. She hated when I came home from work and went straight to my room without interacting with her. She had no one to talk to. Eventually I picked up some of her easy going ways. The best part about having a roommate was that I developed a loving, close relationship. She helped me through some hard times, she encouraged me, she supported me, she told me the truth and she caused me to die to my flesh. She guided me in coming out of myself and led me to do things I would have never done on my own. Because of my close relationship with her, I also learned sincere, Christ-like love for another.

I'm saying all this because this may be a great time for you to share a home with someone who sees you outside the church environment. I am familiar with several roommate situations that completely blessed the women involved. You should certainly be discerning in whom you select as a roommate. I have also witnessed and advised roommates that were going through unpleasant situations. Look for someone that will help you grow, is trustworthy and dependable. A roommate will help expose those areas within you that are not pleasing to God.

There were several moments in my single life of sheer frustration with waiting to be "found." My value and self worth was determined by the attention from men. When there was no one to stroke my ego, I felt inferior. I felt important when someone wanted to be in a relationship with me. I used to believe that a man completed me or that I was significant because someone wanted me. Before long, I came to the full understanding that I was all right being without a romantic relationship. I had to change my mindset, accepting that I was good enough as God created me. I came to the conclusion that a man would be blessed to have "found" me. There were times that I felt lonely, but soon I realized that I was never alone in the first place. When the feeling of loneliness hit, that is when I called on God to comfort me.

I began to watch my single friends get married. Being single and over 30, it was easy for envy to set in. It kept me longing to be with that special someone. I hated leaving church, fellowships, bridal showers, weddings, ALONE. Oftentimes I cried on the way home. Pleading with God, *"When is he going to show up?"* I got caught up in conversations with other singles, complaining about not being married, having the "woe is me" syndrome, not being patient, not understanding what marriage entailed. We had the rose colored glasses on, believing the fairytale.

Marriage is not for the faint in heart. It takes discipline, dying to oneself daily, hard work, confrontation, compromise, and giving when you feel like you cannot give anymore. Deal with the fairytales you have in your mind about married life. Talk to married women to learn what marriage is really like. Life is more difficult and the trials are more frequent when you are married. Not only are you trying to keep yourself sane, you are also trying to keep your family balanced too. All while working outside of the home, managing inside the home, being involved in relationships with other women, working in ministry, and maintaining a close relationship with God.

Stand

This is a tough period for those who have been waiting for a long time for God to send a husband. Discontentment is not the time to lose focus and go into a search for a husband. This is really the time to be quiet and get closer to God. Do not allow your emotional state to cause you to set your sights on someone and develop a crush. Focusing your attention on a new guy at church, the one that smiled at you as he opened the door, is not good. It causes you to create an idol in your life, one that takes the place of God. You have to guard your heart during those emotional moments.

I had a dear friend in my life that had a longing for someone for quite sometime at our church. They used to work together in a professional atmosphere and ended up at the same church. She and I used to talk about this person; someone I did not know. Then, after working together in a ministry one day she revealed to me who he was. I was quite surprised. I sought wisdom from others; trying to figure out if I should tell her that he was already dating. Sometime later the dreaded question came up. She wanted to know if he was dating anyone. I knew, but could not tell her at the time. When I finally answered her, she was disconcerted. She thought that he was the one she would one day marry. I later had to inform her of the woman in his life. It was me.

She did not deal with her feelings or share with anyone what she was going through. Although we still had a relationship, it was insincere on her part, as I later learned. Eventually, she allowed God to heal her heart and deal with her feelings. She and I had a long talk about what took place and what she was feeling. It was a pivotal point in our relationship. Now we are even better friends, able to support each other in what we go through. Fortunately, I am even able to encourage her as she continues in her singleness and share with her my experiences.

Ariana, four years celibate, shared with me that she was concern that she would never marry; wondering if it was God's will for her life. She fears not ever giving birth to her own children, which would be her greatest disappointment. She wants to know if she is really going to live her life as a single person. She feels that if she knew she was not going to get married she could let go of her expectations. Frustration does set in when she thinks of the worldly people that get what they want. Sometimes the thought comes to mind to be rebellious, to cheat and have sex. What she really wants is the companionship of a man, not sex. To hear him say sweet nothings may make her feel good about herself and to know that she still has it. The "it" is being able to attract a man. What motivates her to stand is remembering the mess she went through in the worldly relationship cycle - the drama, emotion and energy spent. She also has the desire to have what God wants for her – the mate that He wants.

Micah is a single parent and also four years celibate. She is at the point of contentment. She stated that beforehand her concern was whether a potential mate be able to accept her and her child, and whether she would ever get married. What motivates her now is the precious moments she gets to spend with God and giving Him her undivided attention. Micah had to keep her focus off of being in a relationship. She changed her perspective when she finally realized that a man does not complete her, she is completed in God. She also realized that even when she is lonely she is not alone. She takes her cares to God. She also changed her perspective of what a husband is – not someone just to have sex with.

Alexandra is also a single parent. She has been celibate for at least ten years. Her biggest concern is actually who God will "hook" her up with, wondering if she would like the person. She does not want him to be aged, or old looking. Although she trusts God, her thought remains on whether she would be attracted to him. The consequences she could possibly face are what cause her to keep moving forward in her Christian walk. She conducts herself as other single Christians and feels that if she does otherwise she would be disobedient. She believes deep down that God will bless her; she has that trust. Alexandra's pitfall is having dreams about someone who is supposed to be her mate. She understands that they are false dreams – fleshly. She also stated that movies, television, and music videos that remind her of past lovers sometime sidetrack her.

These women I know personally. They are mature in their walk and very active in church ministry. I often speak with them to see how they are hanging in their state of singleness. Although, they have a certain level of peace about being single, they still occasionally go through periods of frustration and exasperation. Fortunately, they are well grounded and have close relationships with women who can comfort them during the wearisome times.

Unequally Yoked

2 Corinthians 6:14 says, *"Do not be yoked together with unbelievers. For what do righteousness and wickedness have in common? Or what fellowship can light have with darkness?"* This scripture clearly forbids us not to marry unbelievers, yet some continue to do so, hoping that God will bless sin and change the new spouse into a Christian. Do not be "hard-pressed" or compromise Christian values to marry someone that does not believe in Christ as his/her Lord and Savior. Do not believe the lie that this may be your only shot at marriage, your biological clock is ticking, or that you are not worthy of the "right" spouse; that you should accept sub-standard for the sake of proving to someone else that you are good enough to marry.

A young woman who was in my small group was counseled to break off the relationship with her son's father. He was barely coming to church and half-heartedly honoring his responsibilities as a father. She was often struggling to get money from him to take care of their son's needs. She was also not being very honest or transparent about her situation. She would not share what she was going through until situations blew over. Later, she confided in the group leader that she was going to marry him. She was warned to wait, but went ahead anyway. She is now in a marriage where her husband does not come to church. She goes through trials too often to keep track. She now realizes the impact that her choices have made on her life. She is standing firm, believing that God will turn her situation around for the better.

My warning for Christian women and men, please do not become involved with a non-believer. I am familiar with quite a few stories of women who were Christian and married unbelievers. Some are quite frustrated in their marriage because they cannot walk together in Christ, pray together, or even discuss our wonderful Lord and Savior. Always be mindful that you reap what you sow. If you are currently dating someone who does not believe in Christ, I would suggest that you seek help in breaking free of this relationship. This is not your last hope. Wait patiently for God to bring the husband or wife He has selected for you.

Misguided Ideals

Some of you are antsy and anxious at this time. Some of you are content. Whatever your state, this is a great time to reflect on your own beliefs and standards about men. God knows exactly what you need. Examine yourself to find out if what you are looking for in a man exceeds God's standards. Are you looking for a man with a line up of the following?

- Height: 6'2"
- Weight: 215
- Muscular build: fit with a six-pack stomach
- Teeth: bright smile
- Looks: model-like handsome
- Complexion: dark and perfect
- Personality: amusing
- Job: engineer, doctor, lawyer
- Salary: six-figures

 **The Lord does not look at the things man looks at. Man looks at the outward appearance, but the Lord looks at the heart.** ~ 1 Samuel 16:7b

Do any of those qualities honor God? If not, check them off of your list of requirements. Ask God to change your heart to mirror His on this matter. When you fully submit your desires to His will for your life, when the husband that God has for you shows up, the outward appearance would no longer matter.

Attracting the One

Do you have any qualities in you that do not honor God? If so, allow God to reveal them to you and purge you of these traits. Some negative qualities to be concerned about include:

- Brassy or brash: overbearing, tactless, impulsive
- Loud: noisy or obnoxious
- Controlling: dominant, authoritative
- Vain: self-centered, self-absorbed, stuck-up, princess syndrome
- Overly shy: bashful, reserved
- Selfish: stingy
- Co-dependant
- Temperamental: moody, short-tempered, headstrong
- Independent: self-reliant
- Low self-esteem: low regard for oneself, lacking confidence

Nicholas addressed a few things he believes a woman should work on prior to marriage. His list included providing for yourself all the things you are looking for a man to give, getting your significance from God so that co-dependency does not take root, learning what it takes to be a wife, dealing with bitterness from past relationships, becoming a good steward over finances, and learning the differences between men and women. He even went so far as to describe the type of woman he wants -- one that is comfortable around children, reveres God, discerning, supportive, encouraging, enjoys outdoor activities, desires to grow and is intelligent. Remember, this is Nicholas' list. It may be a good idea for you to relate with wives to find out what qualities that a husband may revere in a wife and work to imitate those qualities. You may also want to begin reading books about the roles of a wife, what a marriage entails and understanding men.

Establish in yourself the characteristics of a Proverbs 31 woman prior to becoming a wife. Here are some suggestions of things you could do:

- Develop relationships with godly, married women who illustrate virtuous attributes and reproduce them
- Learn to clean home properly
- Learn to cook tasty and healthy meals
- Rid your wardrobe of anything that is revealing or sexy that may tempt a man
- Study on what it is to be a wife

Single women with children, this is a time to focus your energies in raising godly offspring. It is better to remain single until your children are out of the home; however, if you believe that God is leading you towards marriage, it is best that you court outside the home, without involving the children. This is to protect them from the getting attached and the distress of disengaging should the relationship not lead to marriage.

If you believe you are ready to receive a mate, establish yourself in a position to accept one. A woman that a Christian man is in search of is one who exudes Christ-like characteristics, is modest in her appearance and temperament, and is in right standing with God and seeks Him wholeheartedly. Are you the one?

Is Your Oil Lamp Lit?

The parable of the ten virgins illustrated in Matthew 25:1-14 reveals the level of awareness and proactive preparation that you should be in the midst of -- for you do not know the day or the hour of your bridegroom's arrival. Do you have your oil with you? For this example, your oil is an intimate relationship with God, the fruits of the spirit, noble character, generosity, compassion, modesty, strength, dignity, watchfulness, household caretaker, lightheartedness, discernment, wisdom speaker, productive and fear of the Lord. During the wait, if you have not yet learned and walked in these attributes, practice and mature in them now so that you may be proficient and equipped when he comes.

Yet Approached

When a man approaches you, God has given you the option to accept or decline. Pray first to find out what God would have you to do. You may not be ready or the man may have come out of the wrong season. Second, find out whom he is accountable to and ask them if he is ready. Know that a decoy can surprise you at any moment. God may be testing you to see if you would follow His lead or will you go your own way. There have been many instances when a man went on his own understanding and did not share with anyone of his intentions. Fortunately, the women were wise enough to inquire about him only to find out no one knew what was going on with him. The women were informed and did not pursue a courting relationship. Last, call on a mature person that really knows you and ask for wisdom in determining if you are actually ready to court. You have to ask the hard questions and be able to receive what was revealed to you by God.

Be careful that you do not go on your own understanding, especially if there is an immediate physical attraction. Know your own emotional temperature. Are you saying yes because you believe that no one else would approach you or that you have been without a man for so long that you are all too excited that someone even noticed you? And so, you jump at the chance to get into any relationship. Watch out. Satan does come in disguise!

Ladies, I admonish you during your time of singleness not to allow your doubt, worries or cares concerning marriage to take you off course. Even if you are approached, please seek God in all you do.

Lifting the Standard

There comes a time in our lives when we need to lift the standards of what is acceptable and what is not. That time came when you accepted Christ. Our old ways must be abandoned and replaced with a new way of thinking. While in the world we readily accepted what we saw others do and accepted what we were told by others. Now, the standards, in the spiritual, physical, emotional and financial realm, should be filtered through God's word. You must be able to discern what is righteous, based upon what God wants for you.

Before you enter into such a relationship, you should have already determined what is considered to be foolish or not. For example, a man approaches you to inquire about beginning a courtship. In being wise, you then seek out those whom he is supposed to be accountable to. They may tell you that he is a great guy, but he still is immature in some areas. He still has not gotten connected to the body of believers in his local church, he still has not joined any ministries and he is in half-hearted relationships with a few peers, only telling them what he thinks they need to know. This should set off the alarms in your mind. A person who lacks connection usually is a lone-ranger. He fights his battles alone and does not seek out the help of others. In his arrogance or pride, he does not heed godly wisdom and does not have a teachable spirit. If he is not truly accountable now, what causes you to believe that he will be so later?

A person that leans to his own understanding usually will not check in with God for direction. The secret is that he has never left women alone. He has low-self esteem and thrives on relationships with women to keep him going. He jumps from one relationship to the next without ever dealing with the issues in his life. He is searching for something, yet he will not knock on God's door to find it. Women pacify that inner longing in him – the one for significance that no one can fill. He has not yet been celibate long enough for God to deal with his heart. He approached you out of season. Would you want this type of man to lead your family?

Another instance to consider includes a man who is desperately seeking validation in things. This man usually is the best-dressed, dapper Dan. He has the latest vehicle with a package that includes expensive rims and the loudest stereo system. Yet, he still lives at home with his mother and does not pay for amenities. He approaches you and what you see is actually what you get. His accountability partners tell you that he is okay, but something should click in your radar. If he does not find his significance in Christ, he will always seek out attention and confirmation from others. In a marital relationship, this will cause great dissention because you will constantly have to be on his case about spending bill money on clothes, shoes, haircuts, and cologne. Your love and respect will never be enough for him. You will always be on guard of the women who flatter him, questioning if he will fall for their schemes of manipulation to pull him away from his vow.

Moreover, you also should be wary of the cool or composed man. His accountability peers tell you that this one has no emotions. Because he is so hard, no one can get in, including God. He may look strong on the outside, but inside he is hurting. He lives in fear of opening up because he does not want to feel pain. His pride will keep him from hearing from God and the spirit of God that is in you. He will keep you at a distance; oftentimes hurting you so bad that you would still love him yet wish not to be around him. He will tear up your self-esteem. His inner vow is that he will hurt you before you have the opportunity hurt him.

If one of these types approached you and it is revealed to you that you should not move ahead, then, let your suitor know that you will not accept the offer and tell him the reason. Do not believe the lie that you have to accept the first man that comes. It is still your decision whether or not to pursue a relationship with him.

Examine yourself and write down those things that are acceptable in one column and in another column, those that are unacceptable. Be sure to base them upon God's view. When he does show up, compare him against the list. You know yourself. Some can tolerate more things than others, but what you are concerned with are your values, goals and purpose for your life. What do you want in a mate and does it line up with what God has designed a husband to be? In addition, check yourself against the list. Do you exude what you want in a mate?

If God say yes, continue to read the subsequent chapters for more nuggets of wisdom.

Career Bound

Some women are intentionally focusing on career and delaying marriage. Nowhere in scripture does it reference women finding a career and focusing on that. Let's speak truth for a moment. I realize our society has greatly changed since biblical times. With each passing decade, our society has also moved farther and farther from God. Even our churches have moved from being God-centered to man-centered. No wonder it is hard not to conform to worldly standards; that is what most of us know.

In the sixties, the feminist movement destroyed the God-ordained role of women. Women were taught that it was slavery to run behind a man, to submit, to work at home and be a mother. We must change our focus. It is alright to focus on a career while you are yet single, but,your views may change once a husband comes into the picture. So get ready.

What I am trying to convey is that I do not want you to miss out in this area because you are solely focused on a career. God does have a purpose and a plan, and part of that plan may include a husband. Yet in still, it is alright to be married and have a career, but a balance must be found. If it is discovered that a career detrimentally impacts family life, the career should be the first to go; not sacrificing the family for the sake of it.

REFLECTIONS

- Do you believe that you are ready for a mate? Why or why not?
- What qualities do you posses that would make for a good wife?
- How would having a roommate benefit you?
- What causes you to become impatient?
- What are your prayers to God?
- What are you looking for in a man?

Spring

Chapter 7

The Courtship

■ ■ ■

Jack Sees Jill, Jill Says Yes

Trust in the Lord with all your heart and lean not to your own understanding. ~ Proverbs 3:5

Are You Sure?

Courting is serious. It is not a time to get to know someone just for the sake of being in a relationship to get your desires met. Both of you should be in a position to marry. Misleading someone causes confusion and pain in the life of the one that has been duped. If you believe that you are ready, but not sure, wait until you are. Moving ahead just to see what happens is not a wise thing to do. A courting relationship stirs up emotions and creates ties. Falsely causing someone to believe that they may be the one when in fact you are just playing the field to see if you like one better than another is dishonest and demeaning. You also must have a goal in mind. This is not a casual relationship. You are seeking to find out God's plan for the both of you.

The Premise of Time

Patience. Patience. Patience. Now is not the time to charge onward full throttled to get to know someone. Avoid getting caught up in the excitement of it all. Remember to keep your eyes on God and not on the prize. The goal of courtship is to become friends with the intention of pursuing God's plan for both of your lives. The emotions need to be contained. It is best not to reveal serious emotional feelings even in non-verbal communication as not to move ahead of God. A courting relationship should cause you to grow spiritually as well in friendship. Henry Ford once said, "My best friend is the one that brings out the best in me." The friendship should be one that encourages, directs towards God, and speaks truth. Your friendship should reflect God's will for your life at this time.

You must be careful not to place a time frame on what God is doing. Allow the Holy Spirit to control the pace of your courtship. Diana put Warren on a time limit. She decided after a few months of courting that if he did not propose within four months she was going to move forward without him. God showed her that she was controlling. She realized that she wanted the perfect picture and decided the outcome for herself. She knew that God was preparing to take her somewhere and He was speaking loudly to her, yet she was still getting in His way.

 **Do not be anxious about anything, but in everything, by prayer and petition, with thanksgiving, present your request to God.** ~ Philippians 4:6

Your relationship is unique and not like any other. Just because other couples courted for a few months or even a year does not mean that you have to follow suit. Allow God to direct every aspect of the relationship and all should be well with you. Nonetheless, if you fail to obey God, there will be consequences.

Time is of the essence. We often put our best foot forward when involved with the opposite gender in order to win them over. We must allow God enough time to remove the façade so you can see the real person you are dealing with. People sometimes conceal past hurts, dysfunctions, and areas that were not previously overcome, such as anger, bitterness, insecurities, fear, past soul ties, inability to confront, etc. Discernment is key during the courting stage of a relationship. You must keep your focus on God and be sensitive to what the Holy Spirit may reveal to you during this time, for yourself and your friend.

Questions to Ask

This is an expansive list of those things you could ask about your potential mate to evaluate their suitability to becoming your spouse and get solid and truthful responses:

Spiritual	
	What makes you believe that you are born-again? What evidence in your life shows this?
	Describe your relationship with Christ and your spiritual walk?
	Are you faithful in your prayer life, tithing and attendance in church and ministry obligations?
	Do you exercise your spiritual gifts?
	Do you have any other beliefs?
	Do others notice that you are a Christian without telling them?
	What are your spiritual strengths and weaknesses?
	What are your views concerning spiritual holidays (Easter, Christmas)?
	What is your life's purpose?
Character	
	What ways do you need to grow before you marry?
	Are you willing to serve?
	What is your faithfulness level to commitments?
	Do you have a teachable spirit?
	How do you relate to authority?
	Are you selfish and to what extent?

Character *(con't)*	
	What causes you to become aggravated, impatient or angry? How do you respond?
	Are you violent?
	How do you deal with broken relationships?
	Do you accept responsibility, repent and ask forgiveness when you fail?
	Do you change when you are found to be wrong?
	How do you deal with confrontation?
	Do you lie?
	Have you ever been in trouble with the law? If so, what did you do?
Relationships	
	Describe your relationships with: Parents, Siblings, Friends, Authority figures, Previous relationships (spouses, girl/boy friends, children's parents)?
	How do you spend your money?
	What are your eating habits?
	Are you materialistic?
	Are you disciplined in studying, commitments, goals, time, personal hygiene etc.?
	What are your habits that annoy others?
Marriage	
	Are you prepared to be a husband or wife?
	What are your views of marital roles?
	What are your views toward women or men?
	How do you make major decisions?
	What do you look for most in a spouse?
	What are your thoughts on divorce?
	How well do you think you will provide for a family or manage the household?

Marriage *(con't)*	
	How will you relate to your in-laws?
	What do you know about child rearing?
	What are your views about family planning?
Miscellaneous	
	What do you do in your spare time?
	What health issues may affect a marriage?
	What are your interest and hobbies?
	Do you like animals and have pets?
	What do you value in life?

Staying Connected

It is important that you not allow a courtship relationship to consume you. You are still single. It seems easy just to focus only on whom you are with at the time and lose yourself in the process. It is an exciting time in your life; however, restraining your emotions is key to a successful friendship. Off kilter emotions will cause you to lose sleep, improperly eat, be distracted from job-related assignments and impact your relationship with God. Normal relationships and activities should continue with the same consistency and fervor you had before you began courting.

All too often we tend to get so caught up in the relationship that we forget we still play a part in the body of Christ. Romans 12:4-5 says, *"Just as each of us has one body with many members, and these members do not all have the same function, so in Christ we who are many form one body, and each member belongs to all the others."* When we fade or drop out altogether it impacts the well being of the body. There is also a tendency to become disconnected from close friends and even those you mentor. Consider this: what if the relationship does not end in marriage? When the courting relationship ends whom and what are you left with? You are left behind. You then have to re-establish your connection with others and the life you lived prior to the relationship. Hopefully they will forgive you and allow you back into their world.

Be careful that you do not become arrogant now that you have "found" someone or have been "found". You have not arrived. Just because a prayer has been answered does not place you above the work of God, your relationship with others, and mostly your relationship with Him. Yes, you received what you desired, but recognize that what God has given out of His free will, He can also take away. Tread lightly in this area.

The one you are courting is not to become your end all. They are not your entertainer, counselor, nor authority in your life. Do not expect them to keep you occupied at all times. They too have a life and should continue it, no matter who entered the picture. You should not expect to go on dates every weekend, do not expect daily phone calls that last well into the night, and do not have them on your mind constantly. You leave no room for friends, ministry work and most of all God.

By the time you are ready to court, most of the mess should have been expunged from your life. Your partner in the courting relationship is not the one to go to for personal answers that you should be seeking from God. Your partner is getting to know the mature you. If this is happening you may be unequally yoked. Both partners should be mature in their walk so that one does not have to be fed spiritual milk.

Moreover, your partner is not your caretaker nor security blanket and you should not be theirs. Do not assume that they will always be there for you. They too have a life. Until God brings a couple into a marital union, the two are still two, functioning separately. Also, you are not to entrust your life over to them, giving them responsibility over your life in your pursuit of validation or affirmation. Do not relinquish control of your life over to them. Your self-esteem should not hinge on what your partner thinks about you. Most of all, they are not your God. Do not place them on a pedestal. When they disappoint you, and they will, you will not be left devastated.

In a courting relationship, your partner is getting to know you and you are doing the same. Allow God to bring the relationship along at His pace. Do not place unrealistic expectations on the relationship. Your life should not be on hold or at a standstill for someone that you expect will marry you. Continue your education, advancing in your career, studying or reading God's word, building and keeping relationships with other singles, staying connected to your local body and the ministry teams you work with and continue to grow in your relationship with Christ. Act as if he or she is your friend. Don't fantasize about your potential future because that is all it is – a fantasy.

Accountability to Married Couples

Also, several married couples should be selected to hold you all accountable. The couples should be familiar with the courting process, know you both pretty well and be able to provide a godly point of view if things get out of hand.

Plans fail for lack of counsel, but with many advisers they succeed. ~ Proverbs 15:22

They should also be able to lead you towards God and away from your fleshly desires. Accountability couples will also be able to detect and expose pretensions of either party. Let God show you whom to select. You must have your own relationship with God enough to discern godly wisdom from the opinions of another. Always check in with God to find out if you are being led in the right direction. Most importantly, stick close with someone who can help you to reign in any emotions, deal with any misconceptions that keep you from letting down your guard. Other singles are not wise accountability choices. There are several reasons behind it, but I will say that you need to discern where they are in there walk, lest you take them off course by your tales of courtship and they may not have any experiences or life learned lessons to help you to make it through the course of courtship successfully. Accountability can:

- Keep you grounded in God: keep your focus off of the fantasy of romance and lead you towards building a friendship
- Help to warn you of trouble before it begins
- Provide you with reality checks
- Provide you with truth

Flesh Reasoning

James 1:25 says, *"But the man who looks intently into the perfect law that gives freedom, and continues to do this, not forgetting what he has heard, but doing it – he will be blessed in what he does."* The so-called rules of biblically based courtship put a damper on those who desire not to be held accountable to their actions. I have heard some people actually complain about the "restraints" of courting. They are concerned about the things they cannot do, they feel restricted, and say that it is too hard. Others complain about courting being legalistic and that courting couples should do what is best for them. These people do not realize the importance of holding oneself accountable to wise counsel. Some have even said that the church way is unrealistic, not comprehending that the alleged church way is actually God's way to help you build a solid friendship, keep you from being clouded by lust or unbridled emotions, and help you not to fall into fornication during the course of the courting relationship.

> **Therefore no one will be declared righteous in his sight by observing the law; rather, through the law we become conscious of sin.** ~ Romans 3:20

Oftentimes, when a couple fails to hold themselves accountable, fornication does take place. I spoke with a woman who is now married, but during her courting relationship she fell into fornication. I asked her if she was accountable. She asked if accountability meant asking someone's permission to do something. I told her no. I explained that it meant obtaining wise counsel before you do something that may put you in a precarious situation. I told her that she was an adult, free to make her own choices, but I let her know that being accountable could help her from falling again. She responded that she was accountable to God. Proverbs 16:18 reminds us that *"Pride goes before destruction, a haughty spirit before a fall."* Reasoning with your flesh and not using the tools available to you to can lead to sin against God, the one you are ultimately accountable to. If your partner disagrees with the principles of accountability, you may need to check in with God and those whom you are accountable to determine if you should continue in the relationship, lest you be manipulated and taken off course.

How Far is Too Far: Boundaries

From the onset of a man approaching a woman to begin a courtship, the man should clearly state his intentions of marriage and immediately set the tone for the relationship. At that moment, healthy boundaries need to be established as well as a plan to follow God's leading. Boundaries that could be set include:

> **Daughters of Jerusalem, I charge you: Do not arouse or awaken love until it so desires.** ~ Song of Songs 8:4

- Limiting phone time, especially late in the evening
- Setting off-limit conversational topics. Such as sex and romance or past sexual history (until necessary)
- Limiting time spent without accountability partners present.
- Abstaining from physical contact (cuddling, romantic touching, caressing, stroking of hair, holding hands, coyly playing, kissing and fornication).
- Avoiding romantic locations such as movie theaters, dark restaurants, and parks.
- Refraining from discussions of future marital relations.
- Being completely accountable for your motives, behaviors and thoughts.
- Setting limits on attire that may be distracting.

It is important that you know yourself and your partner. One thing to consider is what exemplifies love. If it is physical touch, you must be wary and keep your guard up. Do not allow a touch to reassure you. If your partner has that need for solace through touch, you must protect them and not cause them to stumble in this area.

Speak Up!

Proper communication is vital to building a godly friendship within the confines of a courting relationship. As with any friend, you would confront wrong doing, bad behavior, offensive words and insane ideals that do not line up with God's word. Just because the relationship has a different title, does not mean that you treat it in a different way. Keeping quiet about what you see, what you discern and what you find offensive does more harm than good. Both of you will be impeded in the relationship. You may become angry and bitter if you do not deal with your feelings. If you do not speak up, they will not see the errors in their ways. Your friend cannot grow in what they do not know. Since they have not heard anything from you, they will continue to do what they believe is right. You should not fear the person breaking off the relationship if you do speak out. Should they leave, you are the one that might be saved from future drama.

Also, do not assume anything. Speak up and ask if there is something that you do not understand. When you make an assumption, you may believe in a complete lie. Once you believe what is not true, you emotionally react as if it were real. You then may send poisonous words as you vent to your partner, thus deteriorating or destroying the relationship. You disarm the attempts of the devil when you speak up and get clarity. Then you are able to respond accordingly.

I have a set of cards that I keep with me. One says, *"Ask Not, Have Not: If I Do Not Ask, I Will Not Receive. Do not allow fear to keep me from getting what I need or desire."* If you do not share what you would like or what you dislike, you will not receive what it is you desire. Oftentimes, in the courting relationship we do not wish to stir up any trouble or cause confusion. You want to be seen as this meek person who relies solely on God and never needs anything. That is not being real. Sure, you need and want some things that the other can provide. So why not ask for those things?

Lastly, failure to speak up may place you in unsafe situations or areas that you do not wish to be in. You must not be passive by not responding to warning signals. If you feel that any joint activity causes your flesh to rise, speak up and get out of the situation. If you do not, sin may result. For example, you are on a date with another couple, and they leave you alone in their basement. A kissing or sexual scene pops on the television screen. It drops seeds in your spirits to go to a place where you know you do not want to go in your mind or to submit to the pull on your flesh. The smart thing would be to leave. Tell your partner what is happening and set a boundary not to be alone watching television together. Another instance may be when your partner lays on the romance a little thick or coyly contacts you as in continuously bumping shoulders as you stroll together. This is the time to speak out and tell them you are not interested. This may also be the time to revisit the boundaries you both agreed to in the beginning and to talk with your accountability partners. The main point is not to allow your flesh to control your actions.

Andre and I struggled with being on the telephone into the wee hours of the night and while at work. Because we enjoyed conversing so much and were consumed with each other, we let time slip away. Our accountability partners had to rein us in. We decided to be mindful of the time and not be on the phone so late and too much. Do not let romance blind the two of you or allow playfulness to take you both off course. Use your head and not your emotions. Always obey the Holy Spirit's guidance in this area. It will help you to set boundaries in your relationship, prevent inner turmoil from taking place and prevent you from falling into sexual immorality.

Bridled Emotions

During this season it is imperative that you keep your emotions in check. Because men and women progress at a different pace, one must allow the other to catch up. As women, the emotional area is the first level we hit. In order not to either scare him off or propel him to rush forward because of our overly excited and giddy stage, we should refrain from showing the emotions of love. Share with your accountability couple what you are feeling so that they can help you contain the excitement. Because men have been watching for quite some time, they may have passed the physical level and moved into the emotional level by the time they ask the woman to court. Men, you too have to put a lid on it. Your emotions may cause you to move too fast and out of season.

Whatcha Looking For

Anthony's main reason for approaching Jocelyn was that she was genuine; truly being herself. She stood out amongst other women, especially those that were caught up in trying to be found worthy through their behavior. He was certain that he could trust what he saw while realizing that he would get to know more about her later. Overall, Anthony was confident that there would not be any significant behavior changes in the future.

During the courtship phase of the relationship you should be looking for the virtues of a good mate. They include:

- Submissiveness to God
- Honesty
- Integrity
- Secure
- Patient
- Tithe
- Connected with others
- Forgiving
- Self-control
- Honorable
- Unselfish or altruistic
- Service to others
- Contentment
- Caring, sincere
- Trustworthy
- Self-confident
- High self-esteem
- Positive thinker
- Good communicator
- Balanced life
- Good listener
- Perseverance
- Loving
- Reliant on God
- Consistent prayer life
- Imparts wisdom
- Discerning
- Accountable
- Real or authentic
- Transparent
- Committed
- Compassionate
- Courageous
- Empathetic
- Faithful
- Family oriented
- Loyal
- Kind, respectful, gentle
- Responsible
- Supportive

Delaney noticed a serious flaw early on in her courtship with Spencer, however she ignored it. After a while it put a strain on the relationship. He continually withdrew when conflicts arose. The withdrawal was not short-term; it lasted for days. He would ignore her phone calls and other attempts to contact him. His passive-aggressive behavior led him to act as if everything was all right once communication was re-established.

If however, the other person demonstrates the character traits below, be wary and re-evaluate the direction you are headed in:

- Sexually immoral (pornography, masturbation, fornication)
- Manipulation (witchcraft) or controlling
- Abusive in speech or actions
- Hatred
- Habitually late
- Causes perpetual discord or dissension
- Envious or jealous
- Repeatedly withdraws during minor difficulties
- Does not value you
- Miserly - cheap, hoarder
- Grossly overspends – greedy, materialistic
- Unstable – erratic or inconsistent behaviors
- Suspicious beyond reason
- Excessively passive-aggressive
- Prone to anger fits or outbursts
- Lying
- Compulsive
- Unwarranted degree of insult
- Depression
- Disregards feeling, beliefs, decisions, or choices of others
- Inordinately pessimistic

There may be times when the relationship may have to be put on hold for a period of time, or completely dissolved. This should occur when:

- You are completely led by your emotions - no longer being led by the spirit and accepting wise counsel
- Sexual intimacy is imminent due to putting confidence in the flesh and being physically active
- Ignoring what God has shown you – forgetting factors that will hinder your future relationship

- When the other has become an idol to you – no longer focusing on the things of God, but becoming completely attached to and absorbed into the other while losing oneself and relationship with God
- When the person takes up so much of your time that you are unable to live still as a single person
- Jealousy and self-centeredness overtakes the relationship
- No longer being accountable
- Relationship is out of control
- Integrity failure on one or both parties; lack of honesty
- Great immaturity revealed
- God tells you to break it off
- Past hurts and issues not mastered, greatly affecting growth of the relationship
- No spiritual growth on either party taking place
- One or both parties are not ready for a marital relationship

Do not linger in being obedient to the call to end the relationship. This protects both partners from being misled.

Love Verses Lust

Love and lust are not the same. They are very different in nature and behaviors. Lust, as described by Merriam-Webster Dictionary, is an intense sexual desire or appetite; an overwhelming desire; ardent enthusiasm; and to have a strong desire. Scripture tell us in Proverbs 6:25-26, *"Do not lust in your heart after her beauty or let her captivate you with her eyes, for the prostitute reduces you to a loaf of bread, and the adulteress preys upon your very life."* Also, in 1 Thessalonians 4:3-5, God's word says, *"It is God's will that you should be sanctified: that you should avoid sexual immorality; that each of you should learn to control his own body in a way that is holy and honorable, not in passionate lust like the heathen, who do not know God;"*

Love, is a deep-seated affection for another based on relationships; friendly fondness, eagerness, or loyalty; devotion or admiration; unselfish faithful and generous interest for the benefit of another; a romantic episode -- the sexual embrace; the paternal and protective concern for humanity by God.

1 Corinthians 13:4-8a says, *"Love is patient, love is kind. It does not envy, it does not boast, it is not proud. It is not rude, it is not self-seeking, it is not easily angered, it keeps no record of wrongs. Love does not delight in evil but rejoices with the truth. It always protects, always trusts, always hopes, always perseveres. Love never fails."*

- Love is patient, bears all, not hurried, faithful … lust wants immediate gratification
- Love is kind, compassionate … lust is cruel, heartless
- Love does not envy … lust is jealous, spiteful, resentful
- Love does not boast ... lust is prideful; it asserts itself
- Love is not proud … lust withers self-respect and esteem
- Love is not rude … lust is offensive, discourteous, blunt
- Love is not self-seeking … lust is self-satisfaction at another's expense, serves self only
- Love is not easily angered … lust is wrathful
- Love keeps no record of wrongs, forgives, pardons … lust keeps track of mistakes, failures, does not let go
- Love does not delight in evil … lust takes pleasure in the faults, failure or misfortune of others.
- Love rejoices or takes delight in the truth, is sincere … lust is evasive, it lies to get its way
- Love always protects, safeguards … lust cares only for itself, leaves you vulnerable
- Love always trusts, is confident reliance … lust is unreliable, dishonest, deceitful, induces fear or misgivings
- Love always hopes, expects, is optimistic … lust is exudes pessimism, despair and abandonment
- Love always perseveres, is stable … lust easily gives up
- Love never fails or loses strength … lust fades away

Love is a decision to freely give to another, do what is best for another, and sacrifice self-interest for another. If you find that your relationship does not operate in love, but illustrates the characteristics of lust, reconsider the relationship. Pay attention to your state. Know in which of these you are operating in. If it is lust, step back. Check your flesh and put it under the control of the Holy Spirit.

Can You Woo, Woo, Woo

Men, be careful not to overly woo her. If God allows, romance will come later. If you start something that you know you will not continue after marriage, do not start now. If you open the door for her now, you should continue to do so, if not you will cause her to believe that you only behaved as a gentleman just to win her. She then may feel devalued. If you take her to nice, expensive restaurants in the beginning and then McDonald's becomes the fare later on, what signal are you sending her? Do not spend money you do not have. Be honest and let her know that you may not be well-heeled or rich, but you will be able to take care of her should the relationship progress into a marriage.

Women, this standard holds up for you too. Those things like baking cookies, giving small tokens; cards and morning wake-up calls may stir something in him. If you do not cook well, let him know. Not all of us can cook like his Momma. If you normally do not dress to the nines and wear make-up or perfume, do not start now. He should see what he will be getting if he chooses to marry you.

The Process

Usually, a man who is seeking God in this pursuit will have watched a woman that God revealed to him for quite some time before he approaches her. He would find out things about her to see if she is a match for him. In the meantime he is still addressing areas in his life that need to be reckoned with. When the woman is approached she generally has no clue that she has been watched. She is starting at a fresh point whereas he pretty much knows that she is the one. He is at another level. He has passed the emotional stage and is headed for the physical level. She is at first cautious with allowing her emotions to be opened up, she's actually waiting and watching to see if it is real.

Courting is the season of building a friendship with the goal of marriage in mind. It is up to you how you manage the course of the relationship. From my experience and that of others, I will direct you in a way that worked for us. I recommend that the first month or so of courtship be spent with limited time on the telephone. This is the time to get to know the level of spirituality that each person possesses. Your discussion should not be too personal in nature, but limited to what God has done in your life, what He is showing you now, and your relationship with Him, where you believe He is leading you and ministerial service. Other topics may include family make-up, career, education and future goals. It is also fine to discuss your temperament type and personalities. Be led by the spirit. Although you may not be talking about a whole lot, it is important during this time that you hold yourself accountable to someone.

Later, as you get to know each other at a deeper level, discussions can be more personal in nature. The topics include family life as a child and how that may have impacted you, your likes and dislikes, notions of yourself in light of God's view, and other mundane topics. This is also a time for you to find out where your partner stands on some issues, be it political, world issues, spiritual, financial etc. Be careful not to create any emotional ties. You are just getting to know one another. It is important that you begin setting boundaries before you go on your first date. This will guard your heart and protect your personal space.

It is a good idea to avoid talking to a lot of people about the relationship. It should be on a need to know basis. Chit chatting with your single friends is not good. It may stir jealousy in them. Besides, the more you talk about it, the more excited you may get and it may take you to the emotional level too soon. Keep your conversations about the relationship directed to those you are accountable to. In the event that the relationship ends in a break-up you will not have a host of people to explain what happened. You do not wish to go through that, especially if hurt feelings are involved.

Your First Date

Ah! Your first date. Wow, what an exciting moment...or so you think. On my first date with Andre' I was a nervous wreck. I did not know what to wear, how to act or what to do. He called me just before the date to see if I was all right. He was nervous too. This is normal. Usually the man takes the lead by setting up the outing and paying for it. It does not have to be anything expensive. Do what is affordable and comfortable for you. It is wise that you go out with an accountability couple that knows you both. It will be much easier on the nerves when someone else is around to guide you. They can lead the conversation and give you tips on courting. Don't be scared. Enjoy the moment.

As you progress in the relationship of phone conversations and outings, keep your focus on God. Allow Him to steer the course of your relationship. Be mindful of the boundaries you set and stick to them. As the relationship begins to get more familiar, tendencies exist to let down your guard. Be careful, lest you fall. I admonish you not to get into the physical realm. The lack of self-control reveals quite a bit about your walk. It will also be a sign of what your behavior will be like later on. If you are serious about what is happening you will not take someone off course. Should one attempt to move into the physical area, run, they are not ready. The behavior puts you at risk for falling into sexual intimacy.

Moreover, I advise you not to discuss details about marriage that may lead you into fantasizing. You are building a friendship. Courting does not guarantee a marriage proposal. Either party can walk away at any time. You do not want to cause someone to get ahead of you or God emotionally. Your heart will get broken if you do not guard your heart, emotions and spirit.

Courting is also a time for God to reveal to you those things that are inside you that may hinder a marital relationship. When you begin to rub lives with someone, eventually they will get on your last nerve. You may learn that your pet peeves are petty, that some things that you do are truly bothersome and should be dealt with and some of the things you accept are not good. God may also reveal areas you need to mature in. They may include communication, financial management, or relational skills. All of these should be addressed as you get to know your friend.

Consequences: Moving Ahead of God

Caught up in the romance? Are your emotions getting the best of you? Are you no longer heeding wisdom? I once knew a couple that went through a biblically based courtship. They were doing pretty well until they allowed their flesh to cloud their minds. Many warned the woman in the relationship, including her pastor, that she needed to slow down and pay attention to what was really taking place. Everyone else saw what was happening and advised her, but she would not listen and consider the counsel. She went on to marry him despite the warnings. Within a year they were separated. They are now divorced. The relationship not only affected the couple but also the child that the woman had from a previous relationship.

Another woman was in a relationship with a man who half-heartedly and sporadically attended church. She was not accountable to anyone. Some of her closest acquaintances at the church knew she had a boyfriend, the father of her child. They also advised her to discontinue the relationship until spiritual growth took place on both sides. She moved ahead and married him without consulting with others. Soon after they were married he stopped coming to church altogether. Now she struggles in her marriage, trying to fight a spiritual battle with a husband who operates in the flesh.

There are several consequences to moving ahead of God's timing. They could include:

- Losing God's hand over your marriage
- Unnecessarily going through adversity when areas should have been dealt with prior to marriage
- Unable to bring about change in the relationship
- Communication failures
- Temptation / Sin
- Not knowing how to relate to one another
- Inability to make sound or wise decisions
- Lack of negotiation skills
- Lose relationship with others – people will back off of you because you failed to heed godly wisdom. They are not going to help you because they feel giving the wisdom does not bare fruit

Pre-engagement

Courting for more than two years is unwise. Because emotions are involved, if you are not ready, please care enough for the other to not tie them up with you for a few years while you wait to see if they are the one. If you know the person well enough and God is prompting you to move ahead, what more do you need to know?

A deeper emotional and physical attraction should come just about the time an engagement may take place. You may even consider yourself in love with the other. If you are not at this point, take a step back and find out why you are not.

This is a more intimate phase of the relationship. This may be the time to open up more about your feelings, letting your walls come down just enough to reveal more of what you are made of. Do not share anything that you would tell a spouse, for that comes later.

Marriage is a lifelong covenant. Before you plan to get engaged there are several things that should be determined. They include:

- Do you both wholeheartedly believe in Christ?
- Does your relationship honor God and put Him first?
- Does your relationship operate in God-assigned role whereas; the man is the initiator, leader and follows the guidance of Christ?
- Do they bring out the best in you?
- Has spiritual growth occurred in the relationship?
- Have you become friends?
- Are you romantically or physically attracted to one another?
- Has your accountability informed you that they believe you all are ready for engagement?
- Do either of you still have soul ties or current relationships with people that may hinder the marriage covenant?
- Do your future goals include the consideration for one other?
- Are you leaning in the same way for your future?
- Has sexual temptation caused you to move into engagement?
- Have you been through several trails or adversity together and worked through it with the help of biblical teachings, studying scripture, and seeking wise counsel?
- Have you been open and honest with your accountability couples?
- What is your view of the marital roles?
- Do you want to marry?

Walking Away

Evan and Delaney courted approximately eight months. At the beginning, Delaney recognized that their goals and aspirations were not headed in a similar direction. Because he was a Christian, Delaney thought she could overlook it. She hoped that his love for Christ would overshadow the differences in dreams and eventually things would mesh. However, the longer they courted the more she came to realize that they were not compatible in that area. She knew what God had already spoken to her regarding her purpose, and she was not willing to put it on hold or aside simply because Evan did not agree with it. Walking away from the relationship was not hard because she was at peace with her decision. She recognized that she was going to be all right, it was not the end of the world and he was not her last hope. Ending the courtship helped her to know that she could go through tough times and it would not kill her -- she would survive.

If either one of you are having any serious doubts or concerns about yourself or the other, it is time to examine the relationship to determine whether or not you should continue to court. First pray and allow God to reveal the truth of the matter. Next, bring up your concerns to someone you are accountable to so that they can help you weed through feelings of fear, unjustified concerns, or unrealistic expectations. Last, reveal to the other what you are dealing with. Communication is vital at this point. It is important not to keep the other in the dark. This will prevent the other from believing that all is well when it actually is not. Discuss your valid concerns. You may be able to work through this together. The outcome may not lead to dissolving of the courtship, but put it on hold for a brief period to allow you both time to deal with the concerns, have a heart and behavior change, and then come back together as permitted by God. Or, you may find that it is best to walk away from the relationship.

If you or the other do not deal with the deep-set and painful issues from the past as revealed by God, you may end up later living with a "piranha" or "monster," one who will take out their past hurts on you, inflicting never-ending pain or guilt trips. Deep wounds that are not healed will cause you to receive unjust or unwarranted responses to situations that had nothing to do with you. It is best to deal with issues on the front end – before marriage, than to deal with them as they crop up after the marriage, when all madness breaks loose and you have no idea as to what is taking place and how to get out of it. Also, if you both choose not to deal with any voids in your heart, you will then look for the other to fill them and they will become your source instead of God. You will always expect what your mate cannot possibly give you and therefore you are always disappointed and angry because your needs have not been met. Allow God to heal you first so that you do not destroy the marriage before it starts.

Should you walk away from the relationship take the time to deal with your emotions, mourn or celebrate the relationship and assess what took place and determine what you have learned from the experience. Walking away does not mean you are a failure. Learn from your mistakes or things that you have previously overlooked so that you do not repeat them.

If someone abruptly walked away from the relationship without discussing it with you, first ask the other person involved, if they do not respond, then allow God to make it known to you. At this point you can deduce that it is best for you not to be in a marriage where communication is not present. They may have just saved you from a marriage of rejection, neglect and not being taken into account -- a nightmarish marriage.

REFLECTIONS

- Are you monitoring the pace of your relationship? Is it on God's timing or yours?
- Have you continued all activities you did prior to courting? If not, what have you stopped doing and why?
- What is your level of accountability? How is it helping you to restrain from falling into sin?
- Are you keeping the boundaries as set in the beginning of the relationship? Have you added new ones and what are they?
- How is your level of communication? Is it effective in growing your relationship?
- Do you have any misgivings about your partner? What are they and how will you deal with them?
- Are you growing in your relationship with God, spiritual maturity and with each other?

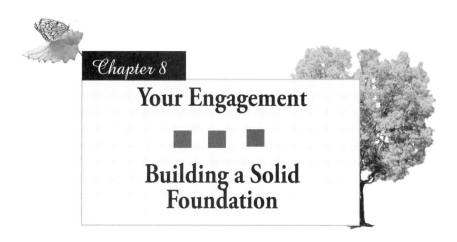

Chapter 8

Your Engagement

■ ■ ■

Building a Solid Foundation

The rain came down, the streams rose, and the winds blew and beat against that house; yet it did not fall, because it had its foundation on the rock. ~ Matthew 7:25

What an exciting time. You are now in a season where it is imperative that you remain focused on God. There is still so much to learn about your soon to be life partner. This is the season when most couples often do not respond to wisdom. Because the overpowering feelings of love can overtake reasoning, it is critical to pay attention.

This is not the season to get romantic and goggle-eyed. You must not be blinded by love, but be awakened to the truth. Do not overlook what you see nor discount the wisdom given to you. It is crucial that you hear clearly from God and obey what He reveals to you. Use this season to study on the intricacies of a biblically based marriage while you are still getting to know each other.

Do two walk together unless they have agreed to do so? ~ Amos 3:3

A lot of things change during the engagement period. You believe that you are now comfortable with each other. You begin to relax, let your guard down. The real you will emerge. The ideal you no longer exists. As you rub lives closer than during the courting phase and spend more time together, things that you did not see are now revealed. You begin to learn more about each other. The things that did not bother you before, when you were caught up in the fantasy now are annoying to you. The good trait of chivalry that he once demonstrated was just an act to win the prize. The ladylike behaviors no longer are presented. The once demure and meek person is gone and the bold and strong shows up.

To Know Him/Her

There are several things that you can do to bring the relationship along and get to know each other at a deeper level. Foremost is one-on-one learning experiences that can help you to grow as a couple as well as in your joint relationship with God. Moreover, helping others during this season is another way to witness each other's interactions with people, reactions to circumstances, and to learn more about individual character. It also provides gifts for others in that you both use your talents to bless them.

Things you can do one-on-one include:

- **Studying God's Word:** this can be done either over the phone or in a public meeting place. Review scriptures that relate to marriage, your circumstances, and help build a closer relationship with Christ.

- **Communication:** choose topics to discuss to see where you stand on specific issues. They can be world related issues such as poverty, famine, global economy, news, leadership, ministry ideas and how they relate to God's view.

- **Workbooks:** there are several workbooks focused on preparing for marriage. Specific areas to focus on include communication skill building, finances, conflict resolution and fighting fairly. Other books to read include those that enlighten you on how to understand and accept a man or woman just as they are created and other marriage related topics.

- **Pre-marital Classes:** attend a session through your local church or search your local area for these informative classes that deal with finances, communication, household chores, roles of each spouse, creating goals and a corresponding time line for those goals.

Instead of just going out on regular dates and being completely focused on yourselves, get out to help someone else. Ideas for events include:

- Feeding the homeless
- Teaching a class
- Reading to a group of toddlers
- Fixing up or cleaning the home of an elderly or disabled person
- Babysitting
- Playing games with others
- Tutor children or illiterate adults
- Grocery shopping for a family in need
- Taking teens to events such as a concert, skating rink, major sporting event, bowling, game playing, etc.
- Taking your accountability couple out to dinner or preparing a meal for them together

To Kiss or Not to Kiss

Prior to being proposed to, I spoke with a few of my married friends and asked them about kissing on the day of getting engaged. I received varying responses, but no conclusive answer as to why I should abstain or not. Well, I kissed Andre the night we were engaged.

It is my recommendation that you save the kiss for when you are at the altar. The reason behind it is because a kiss awakens and stirs up the flesh. I have learned this not only from my own experience, but also from the experiences of others. No matter how mature you may be in most areas of your walk, this area has not been tested in a long while. This area has not been built up and strengthened as others have been. So I say to you, there is no point in trying to see what you can stand or even to test God in this area. You have actually reverted back to a babe in Christ. Set the standard now and choose not to go this route. This is not the time to compromise and put confidence in your flesh. Andre and I struggled in this area until we were finally obedient and chose not to kiss, touch, or be alone in my home for extended periods of time.

Anthony and Jocelyn kissed for the first time one month after the engagement. Jocelyn stated that kissing before you are married will open a door and it is not a small door, it is a huge door – igniting everything. Anthony said it was crazy in that the pull became so strong he wondered if they were going to make it. He also stated that your flesh desires more and more and more, so when you awaken it you should not then say that you would get married next year. After a kiss, it is not wise to put off the wedding for an extended period, lest you be tempted. According to Anthony, from the moment you kiss the flesh craves more. A kiss will almost certainly lead you to letting your guard down. Next thing you know, you will find it easier and easier to go farther – touching, petting, caressing – these set you up for the big fall if you do not rein lust in. When you flow in lust you are not glorifying God. You must have power over your emotions and lustful actions. This will certainly put you in perilous situations if you do not reign in the flesh, set boundaries and stick to them.

A way to set boundaries is to become re-accountable in this area. An accountability couple will cause you to examine yourselves and recommend effective solutions to keep you protected from falling into fornication. Also, prayer is a significant way to combat lustful thoughts, feelings and actions. Another way is to choose public meeting places. Andre' could no longer come to my empty home. We decided not to kiss or hug. We could not spend a lot of time together one-on-one. We were able to pull out of it for at least a few days before the wedding. We kissed, but kept our hands to ourselves. Anthony and Jocelyn discovered that they too could not be alone in certain places. The car was a no-no for them, for that is where they had their first kiss. While at home, Jocelyn's family kept them accountable. They stayed in the living room area or in a room with the door open.

Blended Family

The issue of step-parenting surely may arise for some of you. A United States Census Bureau Study (2000) found that there are approximately 12.2 million single parents, of that 2.2 million are single fathers.

Bringing children into a new marriage poses additional challenges. Your new marriage results in the blending of children, hodgepodge of relatives, and ex-partners. It is not fair or wise to ignore the needs of the children while you carry on with your lives.

Children must be taken into account, as they can either make or break your marriage. They have to make a major adjustment to accept a new family member. It is harder on them especially if they have carried around the fantasy within them that one day their mom and dad would get back together and stay together. They may have concerns that should be addressed and settled before the wedding takes place.

For the new parent to be, it is important that you spend time getting to know the child or children and they in turn get to know you. Invest in them by taking parenting classes or reading books on child rearing and step parenting. Talk with them about the changes that will occur as a result of the marriage. Prepare them for the future. Some children may not be willing to accept the new parent. Don't force them, however, they must be taught to be respectful of the new adult in their life.

As parents of all the children involved, you must come up with a game plan. Discuss how you will jointly discipline, teach and nurture the children. You must be fair to all the children in the decisions made. You cannot treat all of the children the same, because they are different individuals, however, you should not give preferential treatment to one child over the other. This will dispel any favoritism conflicts later on. Discuss potential scenarios as to how you will keep the children from pitting the biological parent against the step-parent. Discuss the following questions and resolve them beforehand:

- What adjustments are you willing to make for the sake of the children?
- How will the step-parent discipline?
- How involved will the step-parent be allowed to be in the lives of the children?

- As a step-parent, are you willing to love and treat the children as if they were your own?
- How will you handle the financial responsibilities when the non-custodial parent is also financially responsible?
- What will be the role of the other biological parent in decision-making for the child if the child lives with you?
- How will you handle child support and visitation issues?
- How will soon-to-be step-siblings be prepared for the new relationship?
- What living arrangements will be made? Will the child have his or her own room if their primary residence is with the custodial parent?
- What are the legal rights of the step-parent?
- Will the child be considered an heir on the will of the step-parent?
- How would you handle your ex's partner's family dealings with your children?

You also have to learn how to effectively deal with the other parent. If the relationship is strained, work toward harmony for the sake of the children. If the other parent is not willing, find a mediator to discuss the terms of the new arrangement and the input the other parent will now have. Be sure to document the agreement so that confusion will not creep up later on.

As the new parent it is a great idea for you and the child or children to jointly come up with a name that the child will call you. This will help the child become at ease with the relationship and gives the child an adjustment period until he feels comfortable enough to call you mom or dad, if he so chooses later on. Do not insist that the child call you mom or dad. Let them make the decision that is most safe for them. The child of one couple chose to call his step-dad Daddy Mark at the beginning of the relationship. After a few years of marriage and he drew closer to his step-dad, he began to call him Daddy. The child's biological father is still very active in his life, so now he concludes that he is special because he has two dads.

It is important for new fathers to take command in your home with the children. They may test and reject you until they fully understand that you are the head of the household and maintain a position of authority in their lives. When you take the step out of step-son or daughter the child will recognize that you consider them your own and will treat them as such. This may be a starting point for them to become secure in knowing that they have a father in their life that will provide and care for them. It will not fill the void if there is an absent biological father, however, it may ease their pain. They will still reap the benefits of your guidance and love.

Expectations

While you are still getting to know your fiancé, it is important that you eliminate all expectations. Do not insist that your fiancé fit into the mold of who you think someone should be. For men who have a great mother that cooks well, loves you completely, cherishes you and does most things for you, do not expect your future wife to do so. She is not your mother. God made her unique -- like no other. She is someone to come along side you as a helpmate, not one to be below you or less important to God than you, nor take care of you as if you were a child. For the women who had an awesome father, one that spoiled you rotten, gave you everything you heart desired, treated you like a princess, daddy's girl, do not expect your future husband to do the same. He too has been made unique, to love you as God designed. Placing expectations on one another only causes animosity, bitterness and anger to develop when they are not met. You both should accept the gift that God has given you. If God accepts you as He created you, then do the same for your mate.

The Engagement Season

This was a hectic time for us. I was consumed in planning for a wedding instead of being focused on building a closer relationship and setting the foundation for our marriage. Our pastor encountered Andre and asked him to get the book _Search for Significance_ by Robert S. McGee. We read the book together. The book helped me to see that if I did not deal with some areas in my life, our marriage would be headed for destruction. I learned that I do not tell my true feelings and had a fear of confronting Andre' to tell him things I did not like or disagreed with. I also was not able to voice any concerns I had nor was I able to tell him what I desired because of fear. I allowed him to do as he pleased, even though I was angry about it. I grew up with strong-willed people in my life that I basically allowed to run over me. I had to learn to stand up for myself.

It all came to a head one day when Andre' wanted to call the whole thing off. I was bothered about some things about him, yet I would not say what they were. After getting wisdom from married friends and being confronted by my roommate, I had to make the choice to confront Andre. I did. I told him what I felt. I also had to tell him that this area was a huge struggle for me and that if I did not change would he still marry me. He said yes. He was willing to stick it out with me until I matured in this area.

Revelations

As behaviors are revealed to you that you find are inappropriate, confrontation should take place. Before the engagement period, neither one of you wanted to rock the boat, but now the one you love is confronting you. Your feelings get hurt when you are corrected. You just did not believe that such a thing would take place. Also, your differences begin to emerge. You learn that the way you do things are not the way the other does things. You have to now accept the person for who he or she truly is and know that just because they do things differently does not mean that it is incorrect. This is the time to really work hard to get to know each other. There are many things you may want to reveal during this season and work together to overcome. They include:

- Past hurts and family circumstances that have caused great pain in your life
- Any family dysfunctions that you may still flow in and discover how it may impact your impending marriage
- Memories that haunt you
- Physical ailments or permanent conditions
- Debt overload

God will also reveal to you any other important matters that will affect your future marital relationship. Be bold and ask God to reveal anything that is in you or your fiancé that will be a hindrance later on. Once you are shown something that is crucial, choose to be wise. Do not allow your emotions to take over -- causing you to ignore the behaviors. If you do not deal with what you are shown, God may arrange your circumstances to the point that either growth in the relationship is hindered or you part ways. You then will have to manage your hurt feelings toward God for doing what He may have orchestrated, knowing full well that it was for your benefit. You will also have to manage your emotions toward your ex-fiancé, while continuing to live life and not be depressed over the situation. Will you choose to respond to God's prompting or will you ignore His warnings? You will either reap benefits or the negative consequences.

Premarital Counseling

There is a popular saying that dentists often tell patients, *"See me now or see me later."* I highly recommend pre-marital counseling with a licensed Christian counselor to help you to deal with issues and start things off right. What has not yet been revealed will certainly be revealed under the guidance of a biblically based counseling organization. Once deep hurts and issues have been exposed, the counselor can help you navigate the healing process and help each other to grow in those areas. If any significant problems have been uncovered, you may want to pause from the relationship until healing or change has taken place, especially those areas that may have a serious impact on your marriage.

Are You Valued?

Being valued in a relationship means that you would not be left guessing what the other is dealing with – concerns, cares or worries. It also includes the other valuing your time and feelings; as in notifying the other of a delayed meeting, not habitually breaking commitments and informing you of their whereabouts. Last, being valued includes leaving no room for misunderstandings. When you leave someone open to assumptions you allow them to go through confusing thoughts and/or unnecessary pain. Discuss everything. If you believe that you are not being valued, discuss this with you fiancé. Find out for yourself what part you play in it, but also, make known that you will not tolerate being dismissed or unacknowledged. If thing don't soon change, you have to make a decision. Will you ignore what you feel, set boundaries or leave? The choice is yours to make.

Should You Marry?

The date has been set, all the plans have been arranged, and the dress and tuxedo have been purchased. Everything is ready except for the couple. Marriage is about oneness -- becoming one in spirit, body and emotion with another. Christ makes you complete. If you have not been completed in him first, you will not find it by getting married. Brandi once believed that marriage would be the end to all of her problems, as in her financial, spiritual, lust and child rearing responsibilities. She later learned that only God could bring healing and true help in those areas.

Do not expect a mate to complete you or somehow make you whole. Your mate cannot heal your hurts, fix your broken heart or deliver you from your dysfunctions. Your significance can only be found in God, no one else. If you place your self-worth in the one you intend to marry, you may need to step back and absolutely find out who you are and your worth in God's eyes.

Two incomplete people cannot make a "complete" union. Two unstable people cannot make a stable union. Two sick people cannot make a healthy union. Should you find yourselves not prepared for marriage or some areas have not been effectively discussed and dealt with, do not be bound by money, schedules, or by people pushing you to get married. The date can be moved until you are both mature enough for the marriage. Do not overlook any shortcomings that you cannot and should not live with for the remainder of your lives. The following is a narrow list of things to consider. Should any of these attributes be predominant in your lives, it may be best to delay the marriage until some growth has taken place. You should not marry when either one of you:

- Grossly lacks self-control in the area of lust, spending habits and temper
- Is in blatant sin or overlooks sin
- Is abusive – verbally, physically, emotionally

- Is still in contact with former boy/girl friends
- Exhibits strong passive-aggressive behaviors
- Is controlling to the point of putting the other in bondage – no freedom
- Lacks a teachable spirit; aversion to authority figures
- Is being coerced into marrying by an outside party
- Exhibits glaring erratic or compulsive behaviors – mental illnesses
- Manipulated the other into the engagement in the first place
- Is overly critical to the point of demeaning the others needs, desires and goals
- Honestly believes that you could change the wrong or annoying behaviors and characteristics of the other once married
- Exhibits demanding and extreme selfish ways
- Compromises against the will of God
- Consistently late – shows a lack of valuing the other
- Withdraws for a long period to avoid honestly dealing with issues
- Does not receive correction, heed godly wisdom, or reacts poorly when confronted
- Is wantonly disobedient
- Habitual liar

Of course we all fall short in some areas of our lives. We all are imperfect. However, some areas should not be disregarded for the sake of pleasing others or the immediate gratification that a wedding ceremony may bring. The ceremony is just an event. The marriage is a lasting covenant. Would you rather get married now and have to deal with the long-term drama or would you rather marry later and have a marriage with short-term growing pains until you all are able to flow as one?

I know of someone who married out of fear of never getting married, fear of never having children and fear of her mother's response if she did not marry the man her mother thought was good enough for her. She was coerced into marrying a man because he came from a prominent family. What the mother did not know was that the man's past is a stronghold in his life. The woman knew of his childhood and how it affected him, but overlooked the potential consequences of marrying a man that was not whole in his heart. The marriage was basically a disaster. Instead of counseling and dealing with his past hurts and issues; alcohol soothes his hurt soul. They both should get into counseling, but at this point, neither is interested in salvaging the marriage. They live together for the sake of the children; however, they carry themselves as if the other does not exist. How unfortunate. If they sought and accepted wise counseling, neither would be in this predicament. Sadly, the children will reap the destruction from their parents.

Once you both are sure the marriage plans should move forward, do not let the enemy try to keep you from honoring the commitment. Sometimes we allow fear of the unknown to keep us from moving forward. Remember, God has ordained the marriage covenant. You have gotten this far with God on your side. He will be with you forever more. Do not fellowship with negative thoughts in your mind concerning whether or not you are capable of being a good spouse for your partner, questioning if the marriage will last, if it will be good, if it would honor God or not. Self-doubt and God-doubt is destructive. Do not make any emotional decisions in response to those negative thoughts. You are a living testimony of God's awesome power. Walk in it and He will see to it that your marriage ultimately glorifies Him.

Moreover, before you marry, both of you should sit down and have a frank discussion about your future. This is a very important time for you to begin dealing with issues that could possibly impact your marriage. Deal with any misconceptions you have concerning marriage. It is time to take off the rose colored glasses. There are several decisions you all should make. The following are some general discussion questions that you should require answers. Set standards based upon those responses and live by them accordingly.

• Describe your dependence upon and relationship with God?
• Are you content in your singleness?
• What do you believe is your role in the household?
• What expectations do you have regarding?
- Overall relationship
- Communication

- Finances
- Household responsibilities
- Shared responsibilities
- Career goals and aspirations
- Children (when, how many, discipline structure)
- Handling disagreements
- Meeting needs or needs being met
• Holidays with family
• Are you able to leave your mother and father to be with another?
• How important is prayer to you and are you consistent?
• Define love?
• Will you be able to seek outside counseling?
• Are you willing to be accountable to other couples?
• What are your personal objectives and desires?
• What significance or importance do you place on the family?
• Are you regarded as responsible or irresponsible and to what magnitude?
• How will decisions be made – conjointly or independently?
• What are your core values and cherished beliefs?
• Are you habitually late and what is the reason?
• How do you behave when crisis hits or you are under stress?
• Are you open to receiving and acting upon godly advice?
• What does forgiveness mean to you and are you able to forgive?
• Are you selfish and to what measure?
• What are your housing desires for the immediate and future?
• How important is personal time?
• How important is time spent with family and friends?
• How important is your personal relationship with God as well as your marital relationship with God?
• What will be the financial structure:
- Who will be responsible for paying tithes and offerings?

- Who will be responsible for bill paying?
- What types of accounts will be set up (separate, joint, savings, money markets, investment, etc.)?
How will financial problems be communicated?
• How important is family? (Parents, siblings, and other relatives), will they be involved in the marriage relationship and to what extent?
• Describe the relationship with your parents and how does it affect you?
• Who is important in your life? (i.e. God, mate, parents, friendships)
• What is the significance of trust in a marriage? What are some of the consequences of breaking that trust?
• What are your fears?
• What comforts you?
• What makes you act out in anger?
• What causes you to become frustrated?
• Are you in close relationships with the opposite gender?
• Do you have any sexually transmitted contagious diseases?
• What is your definition of quality time with each other?
• Do you have high expectations or demands of how you should be treated?
• What are your biggest struggles?
• How do you handle failure?
• Are you faithful?
• Where would you live?
• What type of insurance will you carry?
- Car
- Homeowner and/or renter
- Life
- Mortgage insurance

At the end of discussing all of the questions above and other issues that you deem important, should you discover that many disagreements occur and a mutual understanding has not taken place, you may want to re-evaluate and negotiate some areas of the relationship or seek outside assistance to determine if you should continue the engagement or end it.

On Hold or Calling it Off

Three months before her marriage to Jordan was to take place, Delaney called off the wedding ceremony. She was very attracted to Jordan and their goals and aspirations were compatible. She believed spiritually, naturally and physically that she and Jordan were a good match, however, communication problems existed. Over the course of the relationship, issues would peak from time to time, with resolution; so she thought. She believed that Jordan was aware of the problems and understood her viewpoint. But, the problem would crop up in another form or capacity. Delaney noticed a pattern developing. Each time conflict or a disagreement arose, the same behavior would occur, with varying degrees of reaction. At first she was in denial and blamed herself, believing that the situations were different each time and that she provoked him. Once more, they would settle the issue. Jordan's unwillingness to deal with his issue greatly affected their relationship.

One day, Jordan shut down again, complete withdrawal. He did not communicate with her at all. Finally, she recognized the significance of it and saw no behavior change. She evaluated the relationship and determined that she could either enter into a marriage knowing full well that major communication problems existed and try to fix it afterwards or she could end the relationship and allow him to deal with his problems; hoping to see a change and maybe later they could get back together.

After she cancelled the wedding she was able to clearly see Jordan's heart. All his efforts to get healing in that area ceased. The efforts he made prior to the breakup appeared to be insincere. He was going to counseling to appease her. Delaney knew she did the right thing. She could not imagine marrying him and then trying to push him to counseling. She would have experienced grave difficulties.

When spiritual immaturity in some areas will hamper or cause a relationship to self-destruct, you may need to put the relationship on hold until growth has taken place. This does not mean you simply change the date.

It means postponement without setting a date until all areas have been effectively dealt with and resolved. I will not tell you what is best for you. There are some things you need to find out through much prayer and wise counsel. You need to decide what you can or cannot live with or what you are willing to accept from another. Once the areas have been conquered, proceed as led by God. Should you decide to continue in the relationship, your future marriage will benefit greatly from the growth that has taken place.

You should also be honest enough with yourself to know if there are some things that are in you that still need to be purged from your system. Love your fiancé enough not to pull them through emotional chaos because you refuse to acknowledge and deal with your own mess.

It was difficult for Delaney to come to her decision to end the relationship. She had a ring, date, dress and deposits. However, she made it through ending a relationship once before, and she knew she could make it again. Seven months after the cancelled wedding date, she was doing quite well. She almost felt guilty. She was elated that she did not marry Jordan. She knows of several marriages where one partner overlooked issues and thought that things would change once a marriage ensued or denied that situations were not as bad as they seemed when in fact they were.

Delaney loved her single life. She loved herself and what she was doing. She was not willing to sacrifice her life for the temporary embarrassment that a cancelled wedding could bring. She discovered that had she been dissatisfied with her life she would struggle more with not being married. Since she knows that she does not need anyone to complete her, and though at the time of the cancellation, it hurt terribly, she had managed to continue with her life. Delaney did wonder if she would ever marry since this had been the second relationship that did not make it to the altar. She took that thought captive and found that if she never makes it there, it is not the end of the world.

At one time, Delaney thought that her expectations were unreasonable. People told her that she needed to lower her expectations because she would not find someone to fit the bill. She realized that her expectation was not too high and the bottom line for her was that she was not wrong for expressing what she wanted, especially since it lined up with God. She was not looking for a certain salary or house. In terms of communication, she wanted someone she could sit down with and work through conflicts or disagreements in a functional manner, towards amicable resolutions.

Sometimes a relationship must end. If God is leading you to end the relationship, your only option is to be obedient. There are many factors that may cause a relationship to end; however, God must be the deciding factor. If you choose to disobey God, know that once married, you may live in a difficult situation until growth has taken place -- not because God is punishing you, but because gross immaturity will surely affect the relationship.

The story is not over. Jordan actually worked through his issues and went back to counseling. He later approached Delaney and they began courting again. This time it was quite different. A change in both of them had taken place. They both did all things that were necessary to improve themselves. They dealt with communication issues and resolved problems. They attended a pre-marital awareness class and soon after got married.

The Wedding Plans

Naturally you want to spend a lot of time together getting prepared for the wedding ceremony and reception. Decisions and compromises have to be made. Usually this is when the fighting begins. One person wants a huge event while the other may want a simple ceremony. You may agree on the type of ceremony, but the intricacies and finances may not allow for those little things you want. You may find that your families are incompatible and have to work around them. You have to decide how much input others will have, especially those that may be paying for it. You must communicate and work through all of the issues surrounding the ceremony that may come up. It is your wedding. You do what you want to do as a couple. You are the ones that will relive one of the most joyous occasions in your life and you want it to be a great experience. Start off on the right foot.

Planning for such a huge event in your life will bring out issues that have not been dealt with. How you respond will indicate the flow of your marriage. If you work well together, that is great. But, if you do not, you ought to find out why and resolve the issues before the actual event takes place. As a warning, if you are financing the wedding, be sure that the cost of the ceremony and reception will be taken care of before the event or soon after. Do not let the expenses bound you later in your marriage life.

REFLECTIONS

- Are you headed in the direction that God has planned for you both?
- On a scale of 1-10, how well do you know your fiancé? Are there areas you have not discussed yet?
- How has abstaining from kissing helped you to stand? Has kissing endangered your purity?
- How will you address a blended family?
- What has God shown you about yourself that may hinder a marital relationship? How are you going to improve in that area?
- Has God revealed to you anything about your partner that causes you to take a second look and reevaluate your relationship?
- If God asked you to break off the engagement, are you willing to obey Him?
- Have you planned and paid for the wedding event? How well did you work together to solve issues?

Chapter 9

Marriage Partnership

■ ■ ■

God's Design

Dear children, let us not love with words or tongue but with actions and in truth. ~ 1 John 3:18

God is the creator of marriage. He designed it as a companionship between one man and one woman. Marriage is a journey for a couple to serve out God's purpose together, ultimately to glorify Him and reflect His covenant relationship with His people. The bible gives us a plan on how a marriage should be; it is the ultimate source of authority for direction in the marriage relationship.

> **For where two or three come together in my name, there I am with them.** ~ Matthew 18:20

Marriage, God's way, is the best relationship you will ever have with another human on this earth. There is no relationship like the marriage covenant. It is a gift from God. A gift is anything given freely without expectation of something in return. God gave marriage to his children as a present. When you receive a gift, you offer thanks and treasure what was given. As in marriage, you cherish the one that was given freely to you by God. In cherishing that gift, you take care of it, nurture it, respect it, honor it, revere it, appreciate it, value it, prize it, admire it and esteem it. Your marriage partner, or spouse, is truly a gift from God. God knows you like no other. Because God loves you dearly he will give you exactly what you need. Your spouse is a gift from heaven.

The marriage covenant is a permanent agreement between husband and wife involving promises to each other. At most wedding ceremonies, couples pledge to honor, obey, cherish, respect, love, be honest, faithful and kind in sickness and in health, for richer for poorer, for better for worse, through the joy and sorrow and forsaking all others, keep yourself only unto her/him – a sacred oneness, for so long as you both shall live. They both say, "I Do", seal it with a kiss and the preacher or judge then pronounces them husband and wife. Together they give their word to be equal partners, share life's journey, attain goals and aspirations together, to be helpful and patient with each other, to love unconditionally, accept faults and weaknesses, not allow anyone or anything to come in the middle of the relationship and existing as one for the remainder of their days on this earth.

Inviting God into your marriage, submitting to the guidance of the Holy Spirit and operating in biblical principles certainly produce a stronger foundation. Just as God designed, your marriage will thrive with a Christ-focused, steadfast commitment, and an unselfish mind-set. Ecclesiastes 4:12 says, *"Though one may be overpowered, two can defend themselves. A cord of three strands is not quickly broken."* With God, a couple ordained by Him has the strength to overcome all obstacles that come their way. Your strengths and weaknesses will balance each other out, thereby, producing a powerful unit for God to use in the advancement of His kingdom.

Commitment of Will

A marriage commitment is a promise and assurance to -- continuously carry out the act of marriage according to God's design. It is a resolution made in the mind and then followed by strength of the will to act accordingly. It entails a sacrificial giving of one's complete self. A commitment to your spouse is to leave all things behind; forfeiting dependence on your parents for emotional, financial and decision-making support. Ephesians 5:31 says, *"For this reason a man will leave his father and mother and be united to his wife, and the two will become one flesh."* Consider all things that may have an impact on your marriage relationship such as the place that family, friends, desires, job tasks, volunteer assignments, and relationships have within your marriage.

A commitment necessitates a bold perseverance to stay in the marriage, resolving all issues and conflicts, working together to glorify God and fulfilling God's purpose for your joint lives. When you are committed, you are either spiritually led or impelled as a result of love to "do" for the best interest of your spouse. Philippians 2:3-4 says, *"Do nothing out of selfish ambition or vain conceit, but in humility consider others better than yourselves. Each of you should look not only to your own interests, but also to the interests of others."* When a commitment is broken, trust is damaged. A commitment of will involves some of the following:

- Deliberately engaging in and maintaining weekly date nights
- Investing in your marriage – reading books on marriage, attending marriage conferences, taking classes together, working on marriage related workbooks
- Making your spouse your highest priority
- Meeting their love needs – quality time, affirming words to build self esteem, physical touch, gifts and acts of service (read *The Five Love Languages: How To Express Heartfelt Commitment To Your Mate* by Gary Chapman)
- Supporting God's calling on your spouse
- Loving, despite all odds

Growth Spurts

The season of marriage is also a time for major spiritual growth spurts to take place. When you are rubbing lives this close, iron certainly sharpens iron. God will use your mate to build you up, tear you down, and cause you to become what He has created you to be. You will be hurt, misunderstood and sometimes confused. These trials are designed to bring you closer to God, to each other and to refine you. Your spouse's faults and weaknesses will be used to grow you up. Do not despise them. It will especially be difficult in the first few years as you learn to adjust, put an end to selfish ways and learn how to operate as one. Do not be so thoughtless as to believe that your love will conquer all. God is the conqueror and in Him your marriage will thrive. Without Him, it may perhaps be miserable and/ or fail.

Marital Roles

A function of the marriage covenant is the act of service to your spouse. 2 Corinthians 9:12 states, *"This service that you perform is not only supplying the needs of God's people but is also overflowing in many expressions of thanks to God."* In deference to God's purpose in marriage, we are called to provide assistance, supply the needs and in humility, put the interest of the other before our own. Loving your spouse is a decision on your part, to give without the prospect of gaining compensation. A marriage partnership requires giving of oneself to meet the needs and desires of your spouse. It means that even when you feel like you are at your worst, you should press past it to be there for your mate.

Responsibility of the Husband

Husbands, you are the servant leader. As the head, you are responsible for your family. God held Adam responsible for the events in the garden, not Eve. 1 Corinthians 11:8-10 says, *"For man did not come from woman, but woman from man; neither was man created for woman, but woman for man. For this reason, and because of the angels, the woman ought to have a sign of authority on her head."* God created man to lead.

"He sent dispatches to all parts of the kingdom, to each province in its own script and to each people in its own language, proclaiming in each people's tongue that every man should be ruler over his own household." ~ Ester 1:22

To lead is to be responsible for all that is under your administration. As a leader you must know what you are doing and why you do it so that those who are placed under your care will follow as you move towards the purpose God has for your life and that of your family. As a servant leader, you are to sustain, train, develop and support those who God placed you as head over. As the spiritual leader, you are directed to lead your family towards Christ, in God's word and in your actions. Being the head of the household does not entail lording over your family, being in complete control, dominating every aspect of the marriage, restraining, overpowering or suppressing others. Your wife is your partner, one to be regarded as equal, nothing less. She is just as important to God as you are. The servant leader is not a mark of distinction to beat your chest at, but a function of responsibility and unselfishness. 1 Corinthians 11:3 says, *"Now I want you to realize that the head of every man is Christ, and the head of the woman is man, and the head of Christ is God."*

You are also the provider. The husband is to supply needs and care for his family. 1 Timothy 5:8 says, *"If anyone does not provide for his relatives, and especially for his immediate family, he has denied the faith and is worse than an unbeliever."* Men are created to work in order to provide for their families. As a provider you must be proactive, seeing ahead and making provisions instead of being reactive; responding to a crisis. Be diligent in this area. One of the primary needs of a woman is security. If she is not confident that the family will not have basic needs met, she may become insecure, worried and fearful.

Husbands, in the same way be considerate as you live with your wives, and treat them with respect as the weaker partner and as heirs with you of the gracious gift of life, so that nothing will hinder your prayers. ~ 1 Peter 3:7

Moreover, you are to protect your family. Men were designed to protect and keep everything under its domain safe and secure. This includes safe guarding the hearts of those that your are responsible for, protecting their physical body, protecting and defending the home, keeping their minds from filth, and investigating and analyzing everything potentially harmful to the family.

In addition, you should also teach and nurture your family. As the spiritual teacher, you should be fully versed and operate as an example in the ways of the Lord in order to effectively teach your family. You are responsible for improving the lives of your family so they too can develop into all that God has made them to be. Your family should be encouraged, prayed for, lifted up, directed, and supported and defended.

Last, love your wife. Ephesians 5:25-28 says, *"Husbands, love your wives, just as Christ loved the church and gave himself up for her to make her holy, cleansing her by the washing with water through the word, and to present her to himself as a radiant church, without stain or wrinkle or any other blemish, but holy and blameless. In this same way, husbands ought to love their wives as their own bodies. He who loves his wife loves himself."* The last statement is paramount. Husband, if you prize your wives and they are pleased, know that you too will be pleased. If you sow a good seed, you will reap a great seed in return. A wife who is truly loved by her man will go to the ends of the earth to please him and love him even more in return. I am not saying that it is your job to make her happy, but if you love her as you love yourself, in turn, she will be happy.

Husbands, love your wives and do not be harsh with them. ~ Colossians 3:19

Unfortunately, many women have had to operate as their own provider and protector. Some women are educated and have high paying jobs, established careers and homes. Thereby, allowing them to be financially stable and care for themselves. Moreover, because of the downfall of our society, women have had to take measures to protect themselves. Several are well versed in self-defense techniques, own handguns, mace and other devices to keep someone from physically harming them. Many men wonder what they could do to provide and protect for a women. Women were not designed to handle this area of their lives. So, as a husband it is up to you to operate in your responsibilities in order to free your wife to operate in her god-designed role as a helper to you. At first, you may get some resistance on her part to release these areas over to you. Persevere in operating as her provider and protector and she will eventually let go and allow you to care for her.

The role of a husband may seem daunting, however, rely on the Father, the Son and the Holy Spirit and you will do well as a godly husband.

The Makeup of a Wife

Genesis 2:18 says, *"The Lord God said, 'It is not good for the man to be alone. I will make a helper suitable for him.'"* Wife, you are the one who will support, assist, serve and make life more manageable for your husband. The wife is to come along side her husband as a helpmate – to assist him in every area, to complement, care for, respect, honor, encourage, advocate, counsel and intercede. Proverbs 31:10-31 illustrates the wife of noble character. This wife is valued more than precious stone. Her husband is fully assured of her capabilities. He knows that she has no ill will towards him, she only means him good. She is a worker, getting up early to ensure that her family is fed. She is financially astute, increasing the value of her acquisitions. She is gracious to all. She trusts in the Lord, for she knows her family is under his care. Because of her, her husband is highly regarded. She is strong and dignified. Out of her mouth comes wisdom and faithful instruction. She is vigilant over the matters of her house. This woman reverences the Lord. Proverbs 12:4 says, *"A wife of noble character is her husband's crown, but a disgraceful wife is like decay in his bones."* Wife, it is your responsibility to care for the home – welfare, household affairs, nutritional needs, cleaning, teaching and rearing children alongside your husband.

Ephesians 5:22-24 says, *"Wives, submit to your husbands as to the Lord. For the husband is the head of the wife as Christ is the head of the church, his body, of which he is the Savior. Now as the church submits to Christ, so also wives should submit to their husbands in everything."* The wife out of pure obedience willingly and deliberately submits to Christ in a marriage. The worldly culture makes submission seem like such a bad thing. In Christ, it is what we are called to do – humble yourself before another. Submission does not entail going against God's word because your husband told you to, however, when your husband, as the head, is under God's leading, follow him as we are commanded to do. Submission does not imply dismissing or disregarding your beliefs, opinions or thoughts on a matter. You should speak up when you are aware of something that may be dangerous or bring harm to the family. Submission does not mean that you cannot disagree with your spouse or provide an alternative perspective. A woman's intuition is valuable. Use it. However, do not be insolent when presenting a differing idea.

> **Then when the king's edict is proclaimed throughout all his vast realm, all the women will respect their husbands, from the least to the greatest.** ~ Ester 1:20

Wives, you are to respect your husband. To respect is to show consideration, reverence, value, support, and follow as he follows Christ. Under no circumstances are you to purposely embarrass or disregard your husband. You are not to tear him down with your words or by your actions – operating independently or against his better judgment to get what you want. Constantly arguing or nitpicking with your spouse is also a no no. Proverbs 27:15 says, *"A quarrelsome wife is like a constant dripping on a rainy day; restraining her is like restraining the wind or grasping oil with the hand."* Instead, bring your concerns in a non-accusatory manner and appropriately discuss whatever issues or concerns you may have. Proverbs 16:24 says, *"Pleasant words are a honeycomb, sweet to the soul and healing to the bones."*

Still The One

You are not your spouse. Yes, you are married, but you are still an individual. You are one with a separate personality, characteristic, goals, ideas, etc. You still should be you and not melt or morph into your partner. What you like matters. Who you are matters. What you do matters. Do not give yourself away or allow someone else to take it from you.

Your family, friends and responsibilities are not to be given up because you are now married, except if they affect your marriage. Your spouse is not to become your only support system. You need friends, spiritual mentors, small groups and hobbies to help you. Your spouse is not your girlfriend or boyfriend. Don't treat them as such or expect them to fill the role of one. You lose your self, the one that God created, when you forego who you are and what your purpose in life is when you give it over to your spouse.

Also, do not expect your spouse to be the end all. They are not your God. This is a dangerous thing to do because when your spouse makes a bad choice or mistake, your world is rocked. Only God is God.

Unconditional Love is...

Love is not a feeling. It is an unselfish act, one without conditions. It is a deed or behavior born of purpose to do for another, not based on emotion, but the intentional decision to sacrifice for the benefit of another. There are two types of love. The first is agape, representing an attitude declaring God's nature towards another, expressed out of obedience to God; not expecting anything in return. The other is phileo, depicting fondness, devotion, tenderness, warmth and kindness towards another; it is a give-and-take love. A strong and healthy marriage reflects both.

Love is patient, love is kind. It does not envy, it does not boast, it is not proud. It is not rude, it is not self-seeking, it is not easily angered, it keeps no record of wrongs. Love does not delight in evil but rejoices with the truth. It always protects, always trusts, always hopes, always perseveres. Love never fails. ~ 1 Corinthians 13:4-8a

Love is…

- Being patient with your spouse or situation. Dealing with troubles calmly, without grumbling, exhibiting self-control while under pressure, and hanging in there during the tough times of adversity and being patient with one another in areas of spiritual growth and unintentional oversight.

- Being kind to your spouse and family by being compassionate, sensitive, empathetic, and helpful or giving joy and relief.

- Not envying your spouse or being resentful for something the other has or does -- jealousy, but rejoicing in accomplishments and being supportive

- Not boasting or puffing yourself up, especially at the expense of your spouse, but subtly share the accomplishments instead of putting them down in front of others.

- Not being proud (prideful) by showing extreme self-esteem or by being overly stubborn and not hearing the validity of your spouse's words, but by having proper self-respect and heeding the truth.

- Not behaving rude by being rough physically, emotionally or in your words, not being offensive or abrupt, but by being respectful and gracious in nature.

- Not being self-seeking or selfish to the point that your spouse's needs or desires are not being met or advancing your own agenda at their expense.

- Not provoking anger in another or being so angry that your dangerous response results in harm to the physiological, spiritual or physical well being of your spouse.

- Not to keep a record of wrongs or repeatedly bring up past insults when dealing with a new problem. Forgive and let it go.

- Not to intentionally wrong your spouse by inflicting harm without provocation; violating their rights or will, going against the will of God to suit your own desires at the expense of your spouse, consistently being wrong while fighting for appearance of rightness or being guilty of something and not apologizing.

- Delight in evil by seeking satisfaction in causing pain or discomfort, being morally wrong, or knowingly bringing misfortune or calamity by your choices onto the marriage.

- Rejoices in truth by actually delighting in the fact that your spouse speaks truth to help you and dealing with it in a positive manner instead or becoming mad and seeing it as an insult to your character; facing the fact or reality of the matter and acting upon it.

- Always protecting by shielding from danger (emotional, physical, or spiritual) and maintaining the integrity of the family.

- Always trusting by first being trustworthy and second by relying on or placing confidence in the character, gift, or truth of your spouse; having confidence in the relationship by committing to being responsible for and in the marriage; and entrusting certain aspects of the relationship to another without fear or suspicions, and to extend grace to the other.

- Always hoping or expecting with confidence that your marriage will be successful by looking to the future by setting goals, committing to a plan and following through.

- Always persevering by remaining in the relationship in spite of outside-influences, disagreements, or disappointments by working through issues, investing in your marriage and not allowing anyone or thing to cause the relationship to dissolve. (This is only for those relationships where repeated adultery or abuse does not take place)

- Love never fails when you make the choice to not give up or allow it to fade or lose strength.

Lay Low

During the first few months or year of marriage, it may be wise for you both to reduce your activity outside of the home. This includes church ministries, fellowshipping with others, and reducing job distractions. The reason behind this is for you to build a solid foundation in your marriage. It is a time to truly get to know each other and spend irreplaceable time enjoying each other. Deuteronomy 24:5 says, *"If a man has recently married, he must not be sent to war or have any other duty laid on him. For one year he is to be free to stay at home and bring happiness to the wife he has married."* The time you decide to cut back on distraction is up to you and God. However, I would caution against immediately jumping back into the fires when you return from your honeymoon. If you find that you must be involved, need to be with people other than your spouse, or you cannot work reasonable hours on your job, you may need to check your motives. Is it because your significance still lies in you being involved in everything, believing that you are not replaceable and that people really need you? When you get caught up into the rigors of life, your spouse is left behind and they do not get the opportunity to enjoy or know you. There has to be a balance, even in work for the ministry.

Accountability

Accountability within a marriage is slightly different than that of the courting relationship. Being accountable to another married couple includes wives sharing with wives and husbands sharing with husbands, unless you are having a joint session to discuss issues. Allowing yourselves to be accountable includes giving the couple permission confront you on your behavior. You are also giving your spouse permission to tell on you without the fear of repercussions. Basically, you are sharing how the relationship is coming along and seeking godly wisdom. When situations or problems arise where there is no harmony, an accountability couple can help you to work through the issues, provide a godly perspective and lead you towards mending any tension in the relationship. Select a few couples that have a thriving marriage and are more mature than you both. They should be able to speak truth, direct you towards God and provide unbiased wisdom. Transparency is the only way that this will work to benefit your marriage. When you withhold information and give half of the story, a couple cannot help your marriage. You must be forthright in everything.

Communication

Communication is imperative in a marital relationship. It cultivates closeness, understanding and teamwork. You should feel free to address what concerns you, speak truth and confront issues that are important to you. Hiding in a marriage is not an option. You would not want to be kept in the dark about everyday issues such as, spiritual, emotional, physical and financial matters. It is a must that you get over any fears you may have in coming to your spouse. As a spouse you must be approachable. Your heart should be open to receive what is said, evaluate it and respond in a loving manner.

Successful communication requires that you give the speaker your undivided attention and listen to what is being said. Sometimes you may have to discern the meaning behind what is being spoken. If you are not clear or unsure, speak up and ask that a statement be clarified. Leave no room for misinterpretation. Nothing shuts down or closes the spirit of another more than when they are not being heard. Repeat back what the other has shared to ensure an accurate understanding.

Fear of rejection may be a root that causes people not to communicate effectively. You must know that even if a spouse momentarily severs communication with you, you are not alone nor are you a terrible person. Discern an appropriate time to settle the matter and try to come back together when emotions have settled a bit. It is good to decide together that a matter will not sit idle for a certain period of time. This will ensure that negative thoughts and assumptions will not stir in your mind and Satan will not get a foothold within the marriage. You must be an active participant in developing healthy communication skills.

Trust

The marriage partnership is also about trust. Trust entails complete confidence in the other person. Yes, man will always disappoint you, however, within the confines of marriage, you should have the confidence that your spouse would value you opinion, respect your wishes, lead you towards Christ, and care for your emotional state. To totally get to this point requires maturity of both persons. In the beginning, conflicts may arise in this area. As you grow in holiness and learn what it is to be the best husband or wife for your spouse, trust will eventually fall into place.

Honesty

Honesty is imperative in a marriage. Being honest draws your spouse closer, builds confidence and results in respect for each other and the relationship. Being honest with one another includes speaking truthful about concerns, wrong-doing, mistakes, feelings, shortcomings, joys, pains, delights, inspirations, hopes, dreams, while letting the other know what is going on with you and in you. Honesty reflects the very nature of Christ in your marriage.

Lying breeds distrust, hurt feelings, doubt and anxiety. Lying is making intentional statements to cover up or to deceive. Claming up and not speaking what ails you is also a form of lying. When you do not share your true feelings or concerns the other is not privy to what is actually going on; you are attempting to misinform by concealing the truth.

When one partner constantly lies, deeper issues may be the culprit. Occasionally we are unaware that we lie. We often do this to hide true feelings so that another may not be hurt or to soften the blow. Other times we lie to protect so that someone may not think less or have a negative opinion. Sometimes people lie to mislead others so that their own feelings will be spared. Whatever the reasons, the liar has to make changes so that the marriage will survive. The liar should dig deep inside to find out the reason for doing so and seek help in dealing with the issues.

Dying to Self - Part 2

In your single walk you should have learned to sacrifice for others to a certain extent. However, the marriage partnership takes dying to self to higher level. That higher level of dying to self includes:

- Foregoing an updated compact disc player so that your spouse could buy the dress needed for a special occasion.
- Foregoing the sarcastic comment for the sake of your spouse's feelings
- Foregoing sexual gratification when your spouse is ill or extremely fatigued
- Foregoing eating certain foods that would cause your mate to become ill or stumble from their dietary goals

- Foregoing trips with same-gender friends to spend time with your spouse
- Foregoing gourmet dinners that your mom used to make
- Foregoing personal desires
- Foregoing trips that you would like to take
- Foregoing accepting a job (one that may have a considerable impact on the family)
- Foregoing privacy
- Foregoing certain friendships
- Foregoing your point
- Foregoing winning arguments (at the expense of your spouse)
- Foregoing grudges

If you are not ready to forego anything or only a few things, you may not be prepared for operating in true love that marriage entails. Take some time to mature in this area before you marry. Selfishness will devastate a marriage.

Quarreling / Conflict

Let's face it. Married couples fight. Disagreements do occur. It could be something that seems petty to one, yet is huge to the other. As a couple, you must learn how to navigate through the web of confusion, misunderstanding, and hurt feelings. Not all quarrels are terrible. Some may bring you to discuss an area of importance that had been simmering for a while. The unhealthy disputes come when disrespectful behavior such as, name calling or physical abuse is taking place. This is the time to cool off by departing from the situation. When things get out of hand, you should seek outside intervention; either though professional Christian counseling or through a couple that you have been accountable to. The ultimate goal should be to get to a point where arguing does not exist in the marriage at all and you work through issues in a healthy and functional manner. There are several aspects to conflict resolution; they most focus on effective communication:

- Listen to your mate's concern (focus on what is being said, the tone and legitimate points)
- Be empathetic by placing yourself in their shoes
- Don't take statements personal or become defensive
- See what is behind the statement
- Don't focus on your emotions in response to what is stated
- Ask questions to clarify what is being said
- Repeat the statement so that you fully understand what is being said
- Seek and speak truth, be clear and mean what you say
- Get to the point instead of beating around the bush
- Find out the exact source of the conflict and stay focused on the issue
- Don't bring up past issues unless they are relevant
- Know what it is that you want out of resolving the conflict
- Do not assume anything and leave no room for further misunderstandings
- Confront in love, not to harm
- Know when it is the best time to discuss an issue

Here are a few helpful scriptures to reflect on as you untangle the web of conflicts:

Ephesians 4:26	*"In your anger do not sin." Do not let the sun go down while you are still angry.*
Ephesians 4:29	*Do not let any unwholesome talk come out of your mouths, but only what is helpful for building others up according to their needs, that it may benefit those who listen.*
James 1:19	*My dear brothers, take note of this: Everyone should be quick to listen, slow to speak and slow to become angry.*
Proverbs 15:1	*A gentle answer turns away wrath, but a harsh word stirs up anger.*
Proverbs 10:19	*When words are many, sin is not absent, but he who holds his tongue is wise.*

Ecclesiastes 3:1, 7	*There is a time for everything, and a season for every activity under heaven: a time to tear and a time to mend, a time to be silent and a time to speak.*
Ephesians 4:32	*Be kind and compassionate to one another, forgiving each other, just as in Christ God forgave you.*
Proverbs 21:19	*Better to live in a desert than with a quarrelsome and ill-tempered wife.*
Proverbs 26:21	*As charcoal to embers and as wood to fire, so is a quarrelsome man for kindling strife.*
Galatians 5:22:23	*But the fruit of the Spirit is love, joy, peace, patience, kindness, goodness, faithfulness, gentleness and self-control. Against such things there is no law.*

Pledge to take the necessary steps so that you can successfully resolve conflicts and quarrels. Don't forget to apologize and forgive when all things are said and done.

Forgiveness and Repentance

In order for a successful marriage, daily forgiveness may be required of you. To forgive is to let go of your claim to punish, remind, or carry resentment against your spouse for their unintended mistakes, faults, behavior or deliberate sin. Because God, in His grace, has forgiven us, He commands that we too forgive others. Colossians 3:13 says, *"Bear with each other and forgive whatever grievances you may have against one another. Forgive as the Lord forgave you."*

When we offend our spouse, intentional and accidental, we must seek forgiveness by acknowledging, confessing, and apologizing for our wrong. Then we must repent -- turn away from wrongdoing, defiance or rebellion and return to God.

If the ability to forgive or seek forgiveness is difficult for you, you may not be ready for the daily challenges that marriage brings. An unforgiving heart brings anger and bitterness to both spouses. Ultimately, the state of your marriage depends on your ability to forgive and let go.

Mood Swings

You will face mood swings in a marriage. This is reality. At a moments notice, a spouse may go from happy go lucky to despair, anger, or frustration. An event or thought may cause the one you love to drastically change their behavior. Be prepared. Being proactive in this area means to get to know who you married. Study your spouse. Find out what disturbs them and learn what can help them at that moment. A kind word, hug, kiss or prayer may help diffuse what is disturbing them. Just listening is another great way to help ease the trouble, especially for women. If they do not wish to talk at that instance, be available for them to talk when they are ready. Offer to help your spouse. Just knowing that someone cares can alleviate discomfort or anxiety. Men, it is imperative that you learn about the female menstrual cycle and jot down her behavioral patterns so that you will be prepared for her mood swings. This will certainly reduce marital conflict because you will know what to expect and be able to act accordingly. Wives, men go through their cycles also and you should prepare for that as well by reading up on men and their issues.

Marital Blessings

As the years go by in your marriage, it should become more mature and gratifying. For some of you that may have been scared or alarmed by the previous paragraphs, there are many benefits to being married God's way. The joy of deep love includes having someone to:

- Show you the true love of God
- Bounce ideas off
- Share intimate feelings, hopes and dreams
- Provide support in everything you do, that lines up with God
- Share a life with
- Pray for you
- Comfort you in the times of trouble or discouragement
- Teach you another way to do or see things
- Bring you back to God when you lose focus

- Encourage you in your strengths and help you along in your weaknesses
- Take over when you are unable to
- Encourage you
- Bless you with your desires
- Be your confidant and best friend
- Confronts you in love

A godly partnership allows you to be free to be who you are. Marriage is a huge sacrifice; however, the benefits you reap from sowing good seed far outweigh the growth trials you go through. Remember, the purpose of marriage is to glorify God.

Physical Intimacy

God intended sexual relations as a means to build intimacy within the marriage. One scripture says what you need to know for now. 1 Corinthians 7: 3-5 states, *"The husband should fulfill his marital duty to his wife, and likewise the wife to her husband. The wife's body does not belong to her alone but also to her husband. In the same way, the husband's body does not belong to him alone but also to his wife. Do not deprive each other except by mutual consent and for a time, so that you may devote yourselves to prayer. Then come together again so that Satan will not tempt you because of your lack of self-control."* Just get yourself prepared for it in the spirit, mind, and body.

If you wish to learn more, a few weeks before the wedding I suggest that you read, *The Act of Marriage: The Beauty of Sexual Love* by Tim and Beverly LaHaye. After you are married read *Sheet Music: Uncovering the Secrets of Sexual Intimacy in Marriage* by Dr. Kevin Leman.

To understand more about the marital relationship, there are several exemplary resources available in book format or on the Internet. I suggest that you read them throughout your marriage as a tool to help you grow in your relationship with your spouse and with Christ.

Just Between Us

Wedding vows often state, *"Whom God has joined together let no man put asunder!"* This includes family, friends, co-workers, bosses, ministry heads, even children. No one is to come between you and your spouse. Your marital business is no one else's, unless you are seeking wise council from a trusted mentor, accountability couple or counselor with both partners having full knowledge that conversations are taking place.

It is not wise to seek council from family members, especially a family that is prone to gossip. You do not want your business in the street, nor do you want someone coming back to your partner, telling them what you said. Known problems in your marriage tend to cause family rifts, causing argument because people tend to choose sides in a fight. Should your relationship be healed, they still remember and may not accept your spouse, thereby causing tension at the family gatherings. This also applies to same-gender friendships that are more connected to you emotionally and may not provide good advice, tell you what you really need to hear, or confront you on your own wrongdoing.

Job and ministry responsibilities should not overtake your responsibilities at home. When you find that any type of work impedes the marriage, it is imperative that changes be made so that distance will not grow between you. The changes may include leaving a job for one with fewer demands, altering working hours, or dropping a challenging ministry for one that requires a reduced amount of time and effort.

Opposite gender friends and close-co-workers should not be part of the equation in a marriage. You cannot move away from dealing with the different persuasion, however, developing a close relationship with the exclusion of your partner breeds trouble. For example, going out to lunch alone with co-workers overtime sets you up for either an emotional or physical affair. You may have friends from your past that you remain in close contact with. A relationship with your old girl or boyfriend should be cut off. Do not give your spouse a reason to become insecure and suspicious.

Your children are not to be put ahead of your spouse, period. It is important that your marriage be nurtured. It gets hectic with children's needs and activities, however, you should set aside quiet time just for the parents. Find a regular sitter so that you have alone time. Put the children to bed earlier so that one spouse isn't worn out and has the energy to relate. Do not allow the children to pit you against each other. Come together as a united front in dealing with the children so that their requirements and demands will not separate you from each other.

Where Your Loyalties Lay

Let's be candid. Women are not designed to work eight to twelve hour days in a job and then come home to work eight more hours at home taking care of the house and children. It is no wonder that some women are stressed out, tired, unfocused and lack spiritually.

There is not enough hours in the day for women to both take care of job responsibilities and then come home a be a wife of noble character, one that works with eager hands (Proverbs 31:13), vigorously setting about her work (Proverbs 31:17) -- she's tired. She is not built to do both. She cannot watch over the affairs of the house (Proverbs 31:27).

With all that going on, where do women find the time to be in a relationship with Christ? God designed women to be a help to their husbands, not to the corporate world. Due to the nature of today's society, some women have no other choice but to work. However, when a man effectively operates as the provider and enough is brought in to take care of necessities, women should be able to come off the job and work at home; making the sacrifice to forego keeping up with the Jones' by living a life of material luxury in lieu of earning just enough to take care of the family's provisions and constrained material gain. Imagine a world where all children were properly nurtured and reared in the home by the mother with the father being the provider. Now, I understand that not all women want to come off their jobs to work at home and raise a family. However, if this is something you would like to do, make it known to your husband. If he is in agreement, together establish goals and worked towards them so that ultimately you will be able to leave your job and be a stay-at-home wife and/or mother. Husbands may have to step it up at home so that the wife is not stressed out with work and home responsibilities. You have to work together to create a plan so that household tasks and errands are not overwhelming to one or the other.

Divorce

In this day, it is impossible to tell apart the rate of divorce amongst Christians to that of non-believers. The reason for divorce may vary, but one thing is for sure, that when God is not the central focus, relationships can simply fall apart. When one or both spouses operate in their flesh and not humble themselves to the word of God, the relationship might collapse. It is the responsibility of both spouses to direct each other towards God. Marriage should replicate the covenant God has with his people – His very nature should be duplicated.

> **"Nevertheless, each one should retain the place in life that the Lord assigned to him and to which God has called him."** ~ 1 Corinthians 7:17a

Divorce, by the will of man, legally dissolves a marriage. God did not design the marriage covenant to be severed. Matthew 19:6 says, *"So they are no longer two, but one. Therefore what God has joined together, let man not separate."* Malachi 2:15-16 says, *"Has not the Lord made them one? In flesh and spirit they are his. And why one? Because he was seeking godly offspring. So guard yourself in your spirit, and do not break faith with the wife of your youth. I hate divorce, says the Lord God of Israel, and I hate a man's covering himself with violence as well as with his garment,"* says the Lord Almighty. *So guard yourself in your spirit, and do not break faith."*

In the age of no-fault divorces, people are not taking responsibility for their actions nor are they holding their spouse responsible. Their lament is, "It just didn't work." The self-centered excuses are plenty. They consist of:

- He/she is not making me happy
- He/she is not meeting my needs
- We are not compatible
- I didn't choose the right one, he/she isn't my soul mate

- There are too many conflicts and issues to deal with
- Marriage isn't what I expected
- He/she isn't what I thought they would be
- He/she is too controlling or possessive
- We married too young
- I wasn't ready for marriage
- He/she has changed
- Our finances are in shambles

Now, there are certainly legitimate reasons for divorces such as adultery and physical and/or mental abuse. You have to decide whether you will seek help and remain, temporarily separate until maturity has taken place and then come back together, or completely absolve a dangerous or life-threatening marital situation.

Marriage was not formed so that two people could be completely absorbed within themselves; it is to be God-focused, glorifying Him so that the world would come to know Him through your relationship. It is not about receiving perpetual pleasure but more so about choosing to love; emerging out of obedience to Christ. Part of marriage does entail enduring trials and suffering. You have to decide how you will deal with it in a God-honoring way. Marriage is intended reveal the fullness of God's love and grace, to form spiritual oneness as you grow together while seeking God, and to produce godly children.

We must live beyond the excuses, deal with the root of the issue, and maintain in a marriage as called by God. We need to be better examples to non-believers; especially to those that wrongly believe God does not play a vital role in the confines of a marriage relationship. As God has kept His promises with His people, so we too should kept the promise we made to our spouse and have the same level of commitment to our marriage that God has for us. The following are scriptures that relate to divorce:

Jesus replied, "Moses permitted you to divorce your wives because your hearts were hard. But it was not this way from the beginning. I tell you that anyone who divorces his wife, except for marital unfaithfulness, and marries another woman commits adultery." ~ Matthew 19: 8-9

To the married I give this command (not I, but the Lord): A wife must not separate from her husband. But if she does, she must remain unmarried or else be reconciled to her husband. And a husband must not divorce his wife. ~ 1 Corinthians 7: 10-11

Another thing you do: You flood the Lord's altar with tears. You weep and wail because he no longer pays attention to your offerings or accepts them with pleasure from your hands. You ask, "Why?" It is because the Lord is acting as the witness between you and the wife of your youth, because you have broken faith with her, though she is your partner, the wife of your marriage covenant. ~ Malachi 2: 13-14

Drink water from your own cistern, running water from your own well. Should your springs overflow in the streets, your streams of water in the public squares? Let them be yours alone, never to be shared with strangers. May your fountain be blessed, and may you rejoice in the wife of your youth. ~ Proverbs 5:15-18

REFLECTIONS

Have you read any books on marriage and understanding one another?
Have you learned your God ordained role?
What are you doing to prepare for marriage?
Do you effectively communicate? If not, what hinders you and how are you planning to deal with it?
Have you set goals for your future together?

Chapter 10

Our Journey

■ ■ ■

Spring Has Come

"See! The winter is past; the rains are over and gone. Flowers appear on the earth; the season of singing has come, the cooing of doves is heard in our land. The fig tree forms its early fruit; the blossoming vines spread their fragrance. Arise, come my darling; my beautiful one, come with me." ~ Song of Songs 2:11-13

We truly believe that courting God's way has had a positive impact. What we learned during that season in our lives has been carried into our marriage and has continued to bless us as we walk on to glorify God. Our love for God and wanting to please Him has greatly influenced us. Without God, His word, conviction, truth, wisdom, discipline, grace and mercy we know we will not make it.

> "What makes courting beautiful is the outcome." ~ Andre

During our engagement, our pastor warned us that if we did not slow down and pay attention to the importance of really getting to know each other, we would head down the path of divorce. At that time, we were hanging out a lot and having a lot of fun instead of doing the work of dealing with issues that confronted us. Because we respected his wisdom, we read a book together. The book was *The Search For Significance: Seeing Your True Worth Through God's Eyes* by Robert S. McGee. Andre had read it before. I had not. I learned so much just in the introduction that I cried for the first few days after reading it.

The book was pivotal for us because it taught us that our self-worth was in God and that we were not to seek it in each other. We recognized that God is the only one that can fill the emotional voids in our lives. I could not expect Andre to give me what my parents we not able to give and the same went for him. Had we not read it, we would have driven each other crazy seeking attention and our validation from one another. In essence, we would have made each other an idol. Our normal human faults would have rocked the fantasy that we had and caused us to be disappointed when our expectations were not met.

Accountability was also a key factor for us. Even after we married, accountability kept us, especially in our first year. When times became rough during the growing season, we were able to pull on those that held us accountable for wisdom, prayer and strength as we learned how to operate as married persons. Their insight and experiences, as well as admonition, helped us to become a better spouse for each other. Because of their love for us, they often checked in to see how we were doing. When times were especially confusing and we did not agree, we had a couple that knew us well enough to counsel with us and led us towards God, instead of our separate desires.

Andre's Story – Before I Knew

Prior to seeking a wife, I had to overcome many relational obstacles such as being controlling and selfish and experiencing anger and insecurity. *The Search for Significance* teachings helped me greatly. I liken the study to rediscovering who God is in my life. It helped me to place things in proper perspective in regards to my life, emotions, and the opinions and beliefs of others. Based on this, in the beginning of our friendship I was not looking for fulfillment from Karen in areas where only God could fulfill. I did not put unfair or unreasonable expectations on her; I was free to be a friend.

Because I had realized that my past had demonstrated to me that I did not know what to look for in a relationship, I prayed that I would search for a mate as if I were blind. In that I would not be drawn to physical appearances or other superficial things.

I desired a mate who was not constantly trying to get the attention of others by character or by dress. I searched for humility, a heart for God, His people, maturity, drive, an ability to handle her own issues without being dependant on others, and lastly someone who was ready to move forward themselves and with as little baggage as possible. I'm not saying that it works for everyone, but it worked for me.

I was not sure when the right time to approach Karen would be, so I asked my accountability partner and he told me to just do it; there was no right time. I thought of a time and place where we would cross one another and went from there. I was anxious but not fearful. I did not fear rejection because I knew who I was in Christ. I was anxious because I hadn't approached women in 3.5 years. I didn't really care what her response would be; I just wanted to get it over with.

During the courting process I learned that I still had problems with anger and control. I thought I had grown in those areas, but they had not been resolved. Because no one else had been close to me in the area of an intimate opposite sex relationship, that area had not been work out in me.

Often people function as if God isn't omni-present, this is where I believe accountability is essential during the courting process. I needed this accountability because I was in the process of possibly finding a wife. As a disciple of Christ I had never been in the position of having to search for a wife, therefore, I needed that instruction and guidance during that process. I needed to know that I had the support of fellow soldiers in Christ. Looking back I believe that our courting process went well, but there things that we were lacking. Accountability was there but wisdom wasn't. As a result, we had to experience many different issues first hand. I didn't know what to avoid and what needed my immediate attention.

Courting prior to marriage helped in keeping our friendship intact as opposed to dating as the non-obedient. My goal was to get to know Karen better, not to have sex with her. Courting allowed me to keep the things of God in mind during our friendship and not what I wanted and if Karen could give my flesh what it wanted.

Karen's Story: Before He Showed His Face

Before I surrendered my life over to God, I was in and out of relationships, some lasted a few months, only one made it on and off for a few years. I was looking for someone to love me, but it was elusive. I would not put in the work to make a relationship grow. When conflict arose I ran. When my emotions ran high, I ended the relationship to protect myself from getting hurt. I actually was not in those relationships hoping that one of them would marry me. My concern at the time was whether I was getting my desires met. When I was with a man I felt good about myself. When one was not in the picture, I struggled with my self worth. I believed the lie that a man made me complete; I was important because someone actually liked me and enjoyed my company. I had many male friends; however, some had ulterior motives. Once that was discovered, I moved away from the friendship. I only had one deep female relationship and that was with my best friend. My sister and I were close, but we never dealt with relational issues.

Still, I was busy working and traveling extensively with my job. I was doing my own thing, not relying on anyone because I felt that no one would come through.

The year before I came to Christ, I was searching for something but I did not know what it was. I felt a pull to go deeper into myself and stop doing things that would harm me and others. Because I grew up with Catholic teachings, I actually had a co-worker teach me about the rosary beads. I began reciting the prayer, only to later recognize it was not doing anything to help me. Then, my sister's roommate asked me to go to church with her. On March 3, 1996 I gave my life to Christ. I had no clue what I was doing. I did not understand what had taken place. But being the determined person I was at the time, I decided since I started this, I might as well continue to hang in there. Even as the one that brought me there fell off, I continued on the course.

Seven months later, I found a new church. Initially, I believed that I was a good person and did not have any issues. I soon learned that I thought more highly of myself than I should have and I was very critical and judgmental. I also stayed away from people. It took me about a year there before I actually became close friends with other women. During that first year I was still in relationships with men. I did not have sex with them, but I did kiss and pretty much lead them on. When close calls became a frequent event, I left the relationships. Finally I submitted and decided to leave men completely alone. For four years, I walked without a man in my life. I discovered who the true living God was. I also learned a lot about myself. I became active in ministry, ushering, tutoring, and facilitating a small group. I had even begun graduate school. Through these activities, I rubbed lives with many. I developed close relationships and learned to depend more on God and people, and less on my own strength. My friends confronted and held me accountable to those things that were in me that were not pleasing to God.

I had just been through a spell of sadness and discontentment the week of Independence Day. I attended a July 4th celebration with some friends of the family. There, everyone was paired up except me. My twin sister even had her new boyfriend and was catering to his every need. Envy struck. I felt alone and abandoned by God. Wondering when my turn was going to come and why those that did not serve Him were "blessed." I felt like I was doing everything He required of me. I felt that I was ready and prepared for a mate.

Four days later, after tutoring a child I went to the parking lot and called one of my friends. As I was talking, Andre pulled up besides me, cutting me off so I could not leave. I did not pay him attention. As I was familiar with him because of the various ministries we worked on, so I did not think anything of it. I was on the cell phone with one of my married friends. We were planning to get together that afternoon, just to hang out. After I hung up, I rolled down the window. Andre had been waiting a while. He told me he wanted to ask me something. I responded, "What." He then asked if we could go out on a date. Immediately my thoughts ran a mile a minute. I was in complete shock, not having any clue he had been watching me. I had been "found." I was in a state of utter shock and confusion, I hesitated and then told him I would have to think about it and get to him later.

Ugh! Boy, was I nervous. I called my best friend to tell her. She was quite excited. I was not. Fear had set in. I thought my life was about to completely change. I then called my roommate. She was ecstatic. She laughed at me so much that all I could do was laugh with her. When I arrived home she was rolling on the floor in excitement. I was a wreck. I did not know what to do or say. I then met up with my married friend and told her what took place. She too was excited and ran around the house. I could not bring myself to tell her husband, so she did. He said, *"Cool, he's a good guy."* I was a nervous wreck for the remainder of the day. Later that evening, my close single friend came over to my house. At the time she was deciding whether or not to respond to a courtship proposition. It was great that I had people to talk to that day. It helped me to keep my focus off of Andre' and the potential of the relationship. Because of fear, I was not able to even get google-eyed over what took place that day. My roommate and I stayed up pretty late that evening just talking and laughing about what might be coming in my near future. I would not pray about it that evening out of fear and not wanting to hear an answer from God.

The next day, I went to Sunday service. I was hoping not to run into Andre. I saw his accountability partner. He laughed at me and responded that Andre was a good man. Fortunately I had to leave early due to a cousin's wedding, so I missed the opportunity to run into Andre. I was actually glad. I did not have an answer for him. I prayed that night. Around 4:00 a.m. I awakened from my sleep. I heard the gently voice of God telling me, *"You may proceed."*

The day to respond came. I talked to two of my married friends and my roommate. I knew I would not have enough nerve to call him, so the next best thing was through email communication. My roommate had to wait on the phone and make me email him. I did it. I told him yes and gave him my phone number.

Days passed. My roommate asked daily if he had called. Each day I responded no. Then he called, four days after the email. My roommate and I were watching television and she answered the telephone. She mouthed, "It's him." We then had a wonderful introductory conversation. After I got off the phone with him, something settled in my spirit. I become comfortable with the idea of courting.

Our Courting Journey

We talked over the phone for at least a month before our first outing. Our conversations basically centered on surface areas of our lives and ministry work. We had to get used to the idea that we were able to talk to the opposite gender without feeling awkward about it. It was great learning about each other with no expectations and strings attached. We also read the book *Men Are from Mars, Women Are from Venus: The Classic Guide* _to Understanding the Opposite Sex_ by John Gray. This book gave us many things to talk about as we learned insights about each other. We laughed bout our distinct differences and discussed how those differences may affect us.

One month later Andre planned our first date. I was tense the entire day. We both had to tutor children that morning and seeing him was not of comfort. Later, Andre called to check in on me. I had never been to the Merriweather Post Pavilion so I did not have a clue as what to wear. I asked him what he was wearing. He responded, "Blue." I then pulled out my blue linen sleeveless dress and sandals. I did my hair and make-up, wanting to make a good impression. I looked great. I arrived at the home of one of our accountability couples. Ethan opened the door. He had on blue jeans. Immediately I felt awkward. Then Olivia came out in her blue jeans. The doorbell rang. It was Andre. He had on blue jeans too. I ran and asked Olivia if she had a pair of jeans and tee-shirt that I could switch into. I'm glad she did. I no longer felt out of place.

On the way, we sat in the backseat together. Ethan joked for him to keep his hands off of me. The entire ride was pretty quiet. Both Andre and I are laid back people, not having a whole lot to say. As soon as we got there, we spotted our pastor and his wife. Oh, was I apprehensive. They already knew. My roommate later told me that our pastor said I looked stiff as a board. The date went well. At one point during the concert I was in tears. The jazz music reminded me of my father, who had passed away the previous year. Andre was calm about it. He allowed me my moment.

We then talked for another month before we went out on our second date with a different accountability couple. Each date thereafter had at least a month in between of telephone conversations. At times we were so into each other that we ended up on the phone all day at work and pretty late into the night.

During the entire courting process, my physical attraction was not yet there for Andre. My friends had been telling me all along how handsome he was. I could not see it. I certainly liked him, but I just could not see what they saw in him. Then one day before bible study, he was sitting in the hall. Our eyes met. It seemed like a bright light shone in his face. The veil was lifted. My eyes were opened. Wow, he was very attractive! Later, I discovered that God kept my blinders on so that I would keep my focus on getting to truly know Andre and not be distracted and end up having romantic dreams about him. As the saying goes, love is blind, more like lust. If I had, my flesh would have taken over and I would have been caught up, not paying attention to the important things and dismissing crucial elements.

At one point during our courtship, Andre and I realized that I had many walls of protection surrounding me. I did not allow Andre to get into my heart. I shared this with a close friend. I discovered that I had not yet let go of my father. There was no room for Andre. I needed to go to my father's grave site. I had not been back since the day of the funeral. I felt that if I did, it would all be final, and I was not prepared for that. My close friend, Alicia, told me that she would go to the cemetery with me. The day we decided to go was a beautiful day in October. It was warm and the sun brightly radiated.

I was anxious on that day, more concerned about how I would emotionally react while at the cemetery. I thought I would fall apart. We reached the grave site. Alicia and I sat quietly. Then I heard my name being called. In the distance were crows in the trees. It sounded as if the crows were calling, *"Karen, Karen."* I tried to ignore it. Then Alicia turned to me and said, *"I know you heard what I just heard."* I could no longer deny it. God was speaking through the crows. I sat quietly as God gently spoke to me. He told me to let go and say goodbye to my father. Tears stream down my face as I write this. He told me to go with Andre. I talked to my dad and said goodbye. Afterwards, joy returned. A heavy cloud was lifted. I began sharing with Alicia things about my dad. Sadness disappeared. I was then able to laugh at the good times and thank God for allowing me to have him in my life.

Because that was a very emotional day for me, I wanted to tell Andre about it in person. We tried to set up a date with an accountability couple. It was very short notice, but no one was available. After we gave up trying to meet in person, I told him over the phone. I told Andre that I let go of my father and now accept him as the new man in my life. We both cried. After our emotions settled, we realized that had we been together, we would have ended up physically comforting each other. God protected us. He knew that we were not going out unless someone was available to keep us accountable.

Soon after, I found myself falling for Andre. I called my brother to tell him that I was in love.

He Proposed

I wanted Andre to meet my family. They all heard about him, but never had been introduced. Thanksgiving Day seemed like the perfect opportunity. I asked if he would come with me that day. He said yes. This was our first outing without an accountability couple. Andre met most of my family.

As we were eating dinner, Andre went into the den with my brother. I wondered what they were talking about. Soon after, my brother came into the living room and shouted, *"So, Andre, are you going to take care of my sister?"* I shot my brother a serious look of ire, as I silently questioned what he was doing. Then Andre got out of his seat. I thought he would start preaching to my Catholic family. I grabbed his pant leg to get his attention, have him sit down and be quiet. Andre then began telling my family how he felt about me and what he would not do for me. My aunt started crying. My mother then rubbed on my back. I did not grasp what was taking place. He then got on one knee and proposed. He slipped the ring on my finger. I said, "YES," and then my own tears came. The ring was big, beautiful and radiant.

Later I met his mom and then we went to my home. We sat on the sofa talking and holding hands. My roommate walked in. She had no clue. She asked where our accountability couple was. I then led her upstairs. I put my left hand up to my nose. She saw the ring. She ran downstairs and gave Andre a hug. She was so excited and so were we.

The Announcement

The following Sunday, an announcement was made at church. Our church had a history of playing the song "Another One Bites The Dust," by the rock band Queen, when a man became engaged. Our Pastor asked Andre to come upon the stage. When the song began, Andre asked that Ryan stop the music and play our song. As the song "My Friend," by Crystal Lewis from the Fearless CD resounded, Andre shared his story.

He had been in a church for several years; however, he was in relationships with no intention of getting married. When he came to our church, he did not immediately look for a wife. At that time his focus was on living for God. During this time, God exposed many issues in his life. He first had to deal with his attitude and anger problems. Subsequently he sought understanding and healing with his resentments, controlling behavior, envy and habit of overspending. He then joined the security ministry. This helped him to develop close relationships and to mature into a leader.

Soon after, the pastor asked him if he had he found her yet. At that time, Andre did not know what to look for in a wife. Six months later, he asked again. He still was not focused on finding a wife. As time went on, through teachings and other things, he realized first that he had to deal with himself before he could think about looking for someone else. In essence, Andre allowed God to deal with his heart. Then God opened his eyes and showed him what a woman of God is and what he should be looking for in a wife.

Andre's Perspective

I (Andre) noticed diligence, a work ethic. She wasn't seeking attention. She was just consistent through ministries such as ushering. She's always had her thing together. I was still not taken off course because I knew it was not the time yet; God was still working on me. I began to see her work ethic in the tutoring program. It was nothing she had to do she just had a heart for the kids. I took my time and one day God spoke clear as day that it was time to move. I let my accountability partners, Ethan and Devin know. Ethan asked if I knew who she is. I told him, no doubt.

While he was talking Andre began to walk toward me. Our song was still playing in the background. It was a beautiful moment. My friend was sitting next to me. Both of us had wide smiles on our faces. I tried not to cry. He reached out for my hand. At that moment people cheered, as most did not know we courted and became engaged. I hugged him and kissed him on the cheek. We then walked together hand in hand up to the stage.

Pastor told the congregation how crazy I was when I first came into the church. I thought I was okay, actually believing more highly of myself than I should have. I briefly shared my dating history and that I had been celibate for almost 5 years. The pastor joked with Andre about him being celibate for three years, feeling his head to see if he was okay.

Andre then shared the scenario before he asked me out. As nervous as I was, I went to Ethan, asking when it is time; thinking I would hear a sign from God, "Now it's time to speak." He basically told me that if I was looking for a right time, there is no right time, you just have to step out on that thing, especially when God's already spoken to you. One day after tutoring, I waited for her to come outside for at least 30 minutes. A car cut me off as I was trying to get to her. She hopped in her car then she was on her mobile phone for 20 minutes. I finally was able to get her attention and ask her out. Our lives were then used as an example in the discourse.

During the Engagement

The engagement period was exciting, yet rough. During that time Andre and I got to know each other at a deeper level. It was during this time that we struggled with lust. It began because I kissed him the night we were engaged. It got quite troublesome at times because our flesh was getting the best of us. We knew that we did not want to have sex before we married so we had to reset some boundaries, tell on ourselves, and be more accountable in that area.

We also were dealing with each other's idiosyncrasies. It was also a time when I learned a lot of why I shut down when I am hurt and why I react to certain comments from Andre. It really had nothing to do with him; it was the reaction from past hurts that I had not sought healing and gained understanding. As we rubbed lives on a closer level, I learned other things about myself. Because I had been self-sufficient for a long time, I had to give up or lose control in areas that I did not know how. It was hard for me to ask for something I needed or even allow him to give gifts or do things for me. The dependence that I had on myself was waning and it was quite uncomfortable.

I also began to understand the unconditional love of God. My parents loved me but did not know how to express it. They did not verbally tell me they loved me even though their actions showed it. Consequently, I did not know what unconditional love meant or how it was to be depicted. Growing up I learned that love was based on what you did, not on who you are. When Andre first told me he loved me it was hard for me to comprehend, much less believe. I did not understand my own feelings. As we grew closer and I began to understand true love, I was able to accept things as they were – that Andre actually loved me for me and I did not have to do anything to earn his love. Through Andre, I finally understood what it meant to be loved completely. I was able to connect God's love for me through Andre. He emulated God's love through his words and actions.

Moving Toward Oneness

Although we courted and tried our best to follow God's principles, in no way do we have it all together. In the beginning of our marriage, Andre believed that telling me everything that was wrong about me or what I was doing wrong in his eyes was the way to get me to grow. His constant correction, along with my own insecurities, wore me down. I, on the other hand, was the hider. I kept my feelings under cover. When I was hurt, angry, bothered or frustrated, I kept everything inside. I would not confront Andre. Even though I thought I hid my emotions pretty well, they were still on my sleeve. Because I would not talk to Andre about what I was feeling, he became quite frustrated with me. There were times we walked around our home barely speaking to each other for hours and sometimes days. It took us a minute or two or three to get it together in those areas. Prayer, accountability, wise counsel from our mentors and close friends, sermons and spiritual maturity got us out of that rut.

We also had a hard time dealing with our finances. Because effective communication wasn't there, we struggled in our first year. We had money to take care of bills, it was just that I didn't know what he was doing and he didn't know what I was doing. Andre was also a hoarder. It drove me crazy. It was okay for him to go out and spend a few thousand dollars on a set of surround sound speakers, but when I came home with some books or clothing I got the third degree treatment. I felt like I could not move because I dreaded what he would say. We actually sat down with another couple to talk about the problems we were having in this area. It was a blessing to be able to seek wise counsel from our married friends. After going through Larry Burkett's *Money in Marriage: A Biblical Approach (Christian Financial Concepts Resourceful Living Series)* workbook and class with our church did things change in that area.

We both had to learn what it was to be a husband and wife. We attended a marriage retreat in the fall of our first year that kicked our spiritual butt. The lessons learned helped us a great deal. During some of the sessions we were pretty much forced to deal with our issues. I had to speak up and tell him what I was feeling. We also came face to face with our money management practices. It was sticky in the house immediately after the retreat. We had to confront and tackle the mess we created. Soon after things got better for us, but still things weren't completely in order. I finally became so frustrated and fed up with not feeling like I mattered that I wrote a letter to him and gave a copy of it to his accountability partners. I had to tell on him. I didn't want to do it out of fear of what he would say, but I knew that if things didn't change we would be headed in the wrong direction. Because I did not clearly state what I was feeling, he did not realize what his controlling actions were doing to me. Two of his friends talked with him and from that conversation, his behavior completely changed.

At the time that we married, we believed that we were mature enough and ready. Our relationship was nine months old. In hindsight, we now see that we should have waited a little longer so that more issues could have been resolved and we received additional training in marriage preparation.

Today, we still go through ups and downs. Sometimes it is great and we are living in what seems like honeymoon haven and other times we are getting on each other's nerves. There are still times that we miss the mark. It is a growing process.

Communication is my number one struggle. The problem early in our marriage was that I did not say what I meant when I was bothered or even when I had a need or want. Something was going on inside of me that prevented me from freely expressing myself. I began counseling. It has helped me to understand a great deal about my past and how it has affected me. Now I am learning how to better communicate, deal with co-dependency issues and set boundaries.

Sometimes Andre would take out his unresolved anger from his past out on me in the form of control or utter frustration. He used to get so mad at me for what I perceived as little things, but to him they were major. The pain from his past was unresolved. The blessing is that now he recognizes it, apologizes and makes up for his mistakes.

Most times I am now able to share with him, speak what is on my heart and no longer run and hide when things get too sticky. The apprehension has not completely dissolved when I need to confront, however, the fear of repercussions or rejection has greatly subsided. When Andre does or says something that I do not like, I don't wait to tell him. Even if it is in the form of non-verbal communication, he gets the message.

Andre is currently affirming, complimentary and patient. He guides and instructs with grace, hugs me when I ask and even when he just sees that I need a hug and our conversations are at a profound level. He encourages me, gives me wisdom and allows me to make mistakes; providing me room to grow without condescending words. He is open and receptive when I come to him about my concerns, fears or worries. He listens and supports me; leading me to an understanding that I did not previously have. My love language of affirmation and physical touch are being met. He is operating in his God-ordained role. He is my pastor, my friend, my lover.

We are both learning not to take things personal and recognize that we may be acting out of our past hurts, assumptions and fears. Individually, we are maturing. We are taking the steps to get ourselves together by reading, doing workbooks that help us to deal with our past issues and attending individual counseling so that our marriage will not be affected. Together, we have to ensure that we nurture and invest in our relationship to keep it going. Whenever a series on marriage is taught at church, we make sure we are there. We also take time out of our hectic schedules to spend time alone and check in with each other. Marriage is a growing process, it develops over time. By understanding this, we are no longer trying to change each other into what we want so that we will be comfortable, but are accepting each other as God created us to be.

I enjoy being married. The intimacy, companionship, shared moments, deep friendship and hardships created closeness to each other and to God. I have someone to check my motives, even when I don't like it, but it forces me to consider what I do and make better choices. Marriage has caused us to grow a great deal. As iron sharpens iron, so we too have sharpened one another.

We genuinely love and respect each other. We both encourage each other towards our goals and apologize to each other, work not to mislead each other; leaving no room for misunderstandings or negative thought patterns. We spend plenty of time together, talking, preparing for our future and just enjoying one another. Spiritually, we are both on the same page; having oneness in Christ. Amen!

To order additional copies of
Living in Autmun...
While Preparing for Spring: The Journey Towards Marriage
please contact us at:

The Vineyard, LLC
P.O. Box 478
Upper Marlboro, Maryland 20773

Or visit us online at

www.thevineyard-books.com